HEALING AND REVEALING

*Other books by Bernard Häring
published by St Paul Publications*

Hope is the Remedy
Medical Ethics
Faith and Morality in a Secular Age
Sin in the Secular Age
Evangelization Today
Manipulation
Prayer: The Integration of Faith and Life
The Sacraments in a Secular Age
The Beatitudes
The Song of the Servant
The Eucharist and Our Everyday Life
The Sacrament of Reconciliation
Free and Faithful in Christ
Called to Holiness
Christian Maturity
The Sacred Heart of Jesus and the
   Redemption of the World

Bernard Häring CSSR

HEALING AND REVEALING

Wounded healers
sharing
Christ's mission

St Paul Publications

St Paul Publications
Middlegreen, Slough SL3 6BT, England

Copyright © Bernard Häring 1984
First published in Great Britain November 1984
Printed by the Society of St Paul, Slough
ISBN 085439 238 6

St Paul Publications is an activity of the priests and brothers of the Society of St Paul who promote the Christian message through the mass media

CONTENTS

Introduction

Chapter One: TODAY'S SEARCH FOR A SYNTHESIS OF
WHOLENESS AND HEALING 1

1. Questioning the modern technical model of "health delivery" 1
2. Healthy self-critique of the Church's healing diakonia 4
3. Hunger for wholeness and holistic vision 6
4. Encouraging initiatives 8

Chapter Two: CHRIST THE GOOD SHEPHERD AND
HEALER 10

1. "I am going to look after my flock myself" 10
2. Our Saviour: the living Gospel and the Healer 12
3. Gospel and healing give rise to a saving crisis 15
4. Christ our Redeemer 17
5. Christ: the Reconciler, our Peace 19
6. The Spirit sent by Christ: the giver of life 23

Chapter Three: THE REVEALING –HEALING MISSION OF
THE CHURCH (BIBLICAL VISION) 26

1. Sharing in the redeeming and healing authority of the Servant-Messiah 26
2. Sharing in the redeeming suffering and healing power of Christ 29

Chapter Four: THE CHURCH'S MISSION TO HEAL IN
TODAY'S WORLD 32

1. Proclaiming and making visible salvation in its fullness 32
2. The Church as reconciled and reconciling-healing community 34

   3. The search for life's final meaning: the Church's logotherapy   40

Chapter Five: FAITH THAT HEALS AND SETS US FREE   46

1. The healing power of faith   46
2. The healing power of trust in God   49
3. The healing power of redeemed love   52
4. The saving and healing power of the eschatological virtues   53
5. The healing energies of the sacraments of salvation   56
6. Faith that drives out demons   65
7. Faith-healing   67
8. Healing and liberating reconciliation with death   69

Chapter Six: WOUNDED HEALERS IN A WOUNDED AND SICK SOCIETY   72

1. Dignity and risks of the healing professions   73
2. The "helpless helpers"   75
3. Senior citizens as "wounded healers"   78
4. The family: solidarity of "wounded healers"   80
5. Alcoholics Anonymous as "wounded healers"   83
6. "Wounded healers" and the healing of public life   83

Chapter Seven: THE CHURCH: A WOUNDED HEALER   86

1. The healing power of wounded priests   86
2. A wounded Church in a wounded culture and society   89
3. Healing from a wounded authority-style   92
4. Healing through a healthy life-style   94
5. Healing lepers and being healed from our "leprosies"   95

INTRODUCTION

On the occasion of the beatification of the Redemptorist Peter Donders, the Faculty of Missiology of the Gregorian University in Rome decided to establish a chair to promote the study of the interrelation between communicating the Good News and healing. I am most grateful to the University for inviting me so pressingly to inaugurate this new chair. It gives me the opportunity to concentrate on this important area which, as I see it, has been neglected by theology for all too long.

It is for me a special joy to honour in this way our beatified confrere, Peter Donders. In his long priestly life as an apostle to the poorest lepers, he combined the sharing of the Good News with caring for the sick. Spontaneously he decided to go where human misery cried most pitifully for help. Among the outcasts and the poorest of the poor he felt closest to his Saviour and divine-human Healer.

In the following pages we face the question of what humanity today needs most. My response is: an organic synthesis of the message of salvation and the *diakonia* for people's health, integrity, wholeness and healthy relationships on all levels and in all dimensions of persons and communities.

Such fundamental reflections require a careful diagnosis with the following questions in mind: Where do the main causes lie and what are the chief symptoms of the greatest evils and most damaging illnesses inflicting humankind today? Where do we discover the most hope-inspiring healing forces? What about the healing professions and the prevailing patterns of health-care? How does the Church envisage her mission in this field? Does she realize the need and possibility of a new orientation inspired by the Gospel itself and by present circumstances? Is she on the road towards a new holistic synthesis of sharing the Good News and healing the sick, in faithfulness to the example and mandate of the Lord?

James McGilvray, spokesman for the ecumenical commission which has studied this theme during the past decade, writes: "The

Church, which is the organized and visible expression of Christian discipleship, has always had some difficulty in discovering how it should respond to its Lord's command to heal. In contrast to the other imperatives — to preach, teach and baptize, whose implementation has presented no problems — the imperative to heal has always created some confusion".*

It seems that one reason for this difficulty is that theology has not so far succeeded in incorporating the *diakonia* for the sick as an integral part of the Church's total mission. It has not grasped how intimately and inseparably interwoven are the kerygma of salvation and the healing ministry to sick people, as well as to sick cultures and societies. That they belong together is evident from the core of New Testament tradition of the mission of the apostles, the disciples and the whole community of disciples.

Luke, the physician and evangelist, speaks not only of the mandate to heal given to the twelve apostles but also to that given to the seventy-two disciples. After having brought back to life the daughter of Jairus, Jesus "called the twelve together and gave them power and authority to overcome the devils and to cure diseases, and sent them to proclaim the Kingdom of God and to heal ... and everywhere they told the good news and healed the sick" (Lk 9:1–6). When "the Lord appointed a further seventy-two and sent them ahead in pairs", he instructed them to "heal the sick, and say, 'The kingdom of God has come'" (Lk 10:1–9).

Matthew's gospel is not less explicit about the mandate to heal the sick as an integral part of the mission of the twelve: "As you go, proclaim tthe message: 'The kingdom of heaven is upon you', heal the sick, raise the dead, cleanse the lepers, cast out the devils" (Mt 10:6–7). The closing part of Mark's gospel is highly indicative of the dimensions of the healing mandate, for there it is clear that all the believers are included: "Faith will bring with it these miracles: believers will cast out devils in my name ... and the sick on whom they lay their hands will recover" (Mk 16:17–18). What this gospel says very concisely about the infant Chudch — 'The Lord worked with them and confirmed their words by the miracles that followed"

* J. McGilvray, *The Quest for Health and Wholeness*, German Institute for Medical Missions, Tübingen, 1981, p.1.

(Mk 16:20) — is exemplified in great detail by the Acts of the Apostles.

Later we shall raise the question as to which are the evil spirits and devils to be driven out by the Church in fulfilment of her total message and, above all, which are the ailments and illnesses that the Church is entitled and obliged to heal in fulfilment of her salvific mission.

Acknowledgement
I should like to extend my heartfelt thanks to Mrs Josephine Ryan, now 86 years of age, who for more than twenty years has been so helpful to me in painstakingly typing out and correcting the manuscripts of many of my English publications, as indeed, alert and devoted as ever, she has done for the present book. My thanks go also to Fr William Burridge WF for his work in polishing up my English in this book.

CHAPTER ONE

TODAY'S SEARCH FOR A SYNTHESIS OF WHOLENESS AND HEALING

1. Questioning the modern technical model of "health delivery"

The sheer extent of the scientific and technical advances of medical knowledge and practice is quite breath-taking. The fight against most of the traditional epidemics is highly efficient. Ever more effective medications to combat virus, bacilli, etc., are being discovered. Not less astonishing is the progress in surgery, making possible the transplant of the heart and many other organs. Countless patients in numerous intensive-care units are brought safely through dangerous crises. Hearts that have stopped beating are rendered fully functional again.

However, this development comes face to face with increasingly inescapable limitations. Of these the most obvious and most arresting are the financial demands. The total expenditure needed to implement the present technical medical programme is fantastic, comparable only to the cost of the senseless arms race. Moreover, the advantages of the costly "health industry" benefit only a relatively small minority of the world's population. And the enormous private and public spending on this sector diminishes the funds, materials and personnel that would otherwise be available for preventive medicine, health education, rehabilitation of handicapped persons and effective care for the whole population.

According to various estimates, this costly modern technical medicine reaches not more than ten to twenty per cent of the population of the developing countries. While millions of people are ailing and crippled because of malnutrition and total lack of medical care, enormous personal and material resources are spent on processes that do not foster life and health at all but only prolong the process of dying. This serves no good purpose and benefits no one, and is seemingly only done for the mere satisfaction of technical achievement — and maybe also to quieten the collective conscience of a society in favour of abortion. One has only to think of the proportion — or rather the disproportion — between the expenditure entailed in prolonging the death process and the amount spent on caring for children damaged by their environment or suffering from genetically conditioned injuries.

Behind all these evident facts there are still deeper problems. For vast parts of our populations in the industrial countries the burgeoning health industry takes the form of an idol or, to speak in biblical terms, a demon that has to be driven out. Deceptive expressions are already in current use, like "health industry" and, even worse, "health delivery", implying that health is one among the many things to be bought and sold. People claim a right to "health delivery" from the State, welfare services, or some kind of high-priestly doctors, while at the same time gravely damaging their health by an insane life-style, destructive self-indulgence or by refusing to accept proper responsibility for their own health and that of others. They give no thought to promoting a healthy environment and human milieu. Thus the "health industry" becomes a part of that way of life, that consumerism which increasingly upsets the ecological equilibrium which is already terribly threatened by the industrial-military complex of the super powers and their satellites.

While pestilence is eliminated in some places, in others millions of people suffer from leprosy and similar contagious diseases which could easily be overcome by a minimum effort of human and Christian solidarity. This incredible refusal to rescue people from such terrible afflictions has much to do with a host of different destructive ills which the world of the rich and the consumer society inflict themselves. We have "epidemics" of alcoholism, drug addiction and many other ailments induced by a lack of self-discipline, a spiritual vacuum and the stress of senseless competition. And this goes on constantly, while people look to "health delivery" to cure the ravages for which they have only themselves to blame.

In the so-called "developed" nations, former environmental deficiencies have been "replaced by such unhealthy practices as industrial pollution and personal indulgence in drinking, smoking and overeating ... Efforts to change life-styles which are injurious to health are tolerated, provided they do not bring into question the system which promotes their use under the guise of exercising personal freedom and choice. Hence, people are subjected constantly to the wiles of advertising that encourage them to want and consume more and more, including things injurious to their health".[1] Senseless desires become necessities, and life-styles tend to comply with them.

Having purchased so many damaging things for themselves, the very same people then want to be able to buy health as a marketable commodity available to the consumer society, as an alternative to living a healthy life in healthy relationship with others. The disastrous consequences of this can be measured at least to some extent. Research has shown that this system can be challenged even on the basis of cost-efficiency. "The surveys had revealed that up to half of the admissions to hospitals were preventable conditions."[2] Add to this the numerous people who, for one reason or another, fail to come to our hospitals or are not, or cannot, be reached within the present pattern of "health delivery".

It is not suggested that those people who come with self-induced health problems should not be helped. But the point is that they should be helped effectively to prevent this suffering if the case demands, face up to their own responsibilities for the future. From whom, then, should we expect the most decisive moves: from public health services or from the community of believers?

Sixty per cent of deaths among today's American adults are caused by heart attacks, strokes and cancer. A recent survey of the U.S. National Center for Health Statistics indicates that at least six of the leading causes of death "reflect the state of despair, physiological or emotional, into which our society has fallen. After heart disease, cancer and cerebrovascular disease, the fourth cause is accidents, the seventh cirrhosis of the liver, and suicide comes ninth. Add to this the many man-made diseases which, while not fatal, blight the lives of their victims. Doctors tell us frankly: "It is our deliberately chosen and cultivated western life-style — what we eat, drink and smoke — that causes most illnesses".[3]

The prevailing scientific-technical medical model is so one-sidedly busy repairing bodily disfunctions and defects that it becomes blind to the deeper cultural, social and spiritual situations that make so many people pitiably ill. In this situation we look to the findings of new anthropological schools of medicine, to the psycho-somatic medicines and to the insights of various schools of psychotherapy.

But while there are encouraging beginnings, a certain turn to a holistic vision and therapy, we must face the sad reality that the prevailing trends in clinical psychology are still far away from a healthy vision. A. E. Bergin has studied thirty leading textbooks on clinical psychology (psychotherapy) and found that they do not even mention "God" or the "spiritual dimensions" of man. While they claim to study and act on the basis of a "value-free" approach, they are far from being neutral; they are actually inimical to the holistic vision which includes a theistic conviction.[4] How, then, can they restore people to wholeness?

On an empirical level we can already see how wrong this trend is. It has been shown that Mormons in Utah have thirty per cent less incidence of cancer than the rest of the population. Regular churchgoers in Washington County, Maryland, have forty per cent less risk of arteriosclerotic heart diseases. These and many other obesrvations lead outstanding doctors and many alert Christians to question the prevailing model of health care. They ask what kind of self-understanding of man it implies: is Descartes' dichotomy, which severed soul from the body-machine, still operative? Whose employee is the healing profession within this technical-scientific model? Whose interests are served? What are the limits within which this model can still render service?

2. Healthy self-critique of the Church's healing diakonia

There can be no doubt that the Church makes a major contribution to human health. To a great extent this comes as an indirect but precious consequence of reconciliation with God, with oneself and with one's neighbour, and from basic education for responsibility and co-responsibility. But the Christian Churches of today are beginning to ask themselves radically whether they have in fact been fulfilling the divine mandate to heal the sick in complete integration with the ministry of salvation and to meet today's urgent needs.

There are some points on which most might agree: 1) in the theological formation given to recent generations, little or no attention has been devoted to the Lord's mandate for the Church to heal the sick as an essential part of her mission; 2) in the manuals of moral theology and specific treatises on medical ethics the prevailing approach has been one of casuistry. In keeping with the approach of modern medicine, it dealt with sick organs rather than with the sick person see has a whole human being. Therapy was for damaged organs (not only where sexual organs were concerned) rather than for the psychosomatic-spiritual health of the person. The underlying anthropology was more that of Descartes than of the Bible and the best holistic anthropology of today. In other words, Catholic medical ethics did not query the basic assumptions of the anthropology on which the modern technical medical model is built. It did not discern the "spirit of the era" and, therefore, was unable to read the "signs of the times"; 3) the missionary and charitable élan of the Churches along with missiology generously promoted institutes for medical missions and for marvellous medical activity in mission countries. What has been done in the service of the sick deserves unreserved admiration. But for a long time not enough study was given to the meaning and role of healing within the indivisible mandate given to the Church to proclaim the message of salvation and to heal.

Today there is a growing awareness, especially within the World Council of Churches and within the faculties of missiology, that the healing ministry of the Church can be understood and faithfully fulfilled only within a biblical and anthropological synthesis of the ministry of salvation, and that this has to be taken very seriously, not only for the sake of effective healing but equally for the fulfilment of the proclamation and celebration of salvation.

It must be acknowledged that the Christian missions have done much for medical education and for the most pressing needs of the poor in the area of each mission station. Special mention is deserved by the missionary medical sisters and other nurses who have reached large numbers of families in their dispensaries. Lately there has been a healthy development of "community medicine" in at least some mission countries. But, by and large, the efforts of these dedicated missionaries and lay-helpers have concentrated on hospitals and clinics. As early as 1910, the Evangelical Churches were supporting 2,100 hospitals and 4,000 clinics in mission countries. Little by little the Catholic missions reached the same level and even surpassed it.

The chief weakness was probably that mission hospitals and clinics generally followed the modern technical medical model. Because of later explosive increases in the cost of this type of institution, even the poor had to pay in order to keep them functioning. Thus, hospitals originally erected for the poor had to serve the privileged class more than the very poor.

As far as the Protestant missions are concerned, James Gilvray notes that "Ninety-five per cent of the Churches' medical activities were focused around the curative services in hospitals and clinics. Very little was done to promote health or prevent disease".[5] I think that the Catholic missions have not shown quite the same disproportion, at least not during the past decade.

The new approach, promoted by the World Council of Churches and also within the Catholic Church, focuses much more on preventive medicine and general health education. Much is done, and more is still to be done, to overcome the inherited individualism. The Church as a whole and each community has to be seen as and transformed into a "healing community".[6]

Through the integrated ministry of the Church, people should learn what truly human health means and how each person and each community can promote health and healthy, healing relationships and conditions of life. But we should also learn how to discover in illness and suffering a deeper meaning, and how to heal what can be healed and deal creatively with the rest. This, too, is part of truly human health in the light of redemption.

3. Hunger for wholeness and holistic vision

The best thinkers on this subject still feel strongly that there is nothing more greatly needed by our sick people and sick culture than "the spirit of wholeness" (title of a book signed with the pseudonym, "Der Rembrandt-Deutsche"). Not only for modern medicine but also for a considerable part of modern art the diagnosis was: "loss of wholeness", "loss of the spiritual centre" (H. Sedlmayer).

One of the deepest causes of the crisis in modern medicine, and especially in the modern technical medical model, is a one-sided differentiation and specialization which, almost unavoidably, results in a blocked vision of wholeness. "Differentiation is the cutting edge of the modernization process, sundering cruelly what tradition had joined ... Differentiation slices through ancient primordial ties and identities, leaving crisis and 'wholeness-hunger' in its wake".[7]

In no area of human life is the loss of holistic vision so devastating as in the field of religion and health. The English word "health" comes from the same root, *hal*, as "whole" and "holy". The same affinity is found in the German *heil*, *helig*, *heilen*, *heil-sein*. The holistic expression *salus* of the Latin language is the origin of the Italian *salvezza* (salvation) and *salute* (health). Thus etymology itself indicates that salvation and health are inter-related and can be understood only in a holistic vision, though that does call for careful distinctions.

Modern medicine deals with not only a variety of functions but also a variety of dimensions and levels. Surgery deals with physical functions and organs — at least primarily; medicative treatment works at the level of chemistry; psychoanalysis and psychotherapy operate on the psychic level (self-awareness, perception and so on); logotherapy gives priority to the spiritual dimension. Social medicine and sociology of medicine emphasize human relationships, the interrelation of health and sickness with social processes, structures and the like. There is sharp awareness of the inter-relatedness of the sick person and sick society, culture, and so on.

Modern medicine developed in the context of modern science, and progressed thanks to scientific method. It adopted most of the assumptions taken for granted by modern natural sciences. It was almost normal for it to overlook the spiritual dimension of mankind or to exclude it categorically. The consequences of this were all the more disastrous because even the dimension of psychosomatic wholeness was being neglected or ignored. An experienced physician rightly remarks: "The religious dimension can be ignored, but it is ignored only with loss to both patient and physician".[8]

It is one of the positive signs of our time that more and more physicians and professors of medicine are becoming aware of the "hunger for wholeness'. Many factors have contributed to this new development. Martin Marty remarks: "Medicine, once sure of its scientific future, is becoming more open to holistic inquiry, thanks to pressure from patients, outside criticism, and second thoughts by medical and health professionals".[9]

The same holds true in a large measure for theology and missiology. There is a new awareness of the need for inter-disciplinary research and reflection, based on a new holistic vision which requires the co-operation of the various competences. As the insight dawns in some circles of scientists and doctors that health and sickness cannot really be understood if the dimensions of salvation and wholeness are ignored, so, too, theologians are beginning to realize that they will inevitably fall short of a holistic vision of man unless all the insights of the various disciplines that go to the study of the human person and the conditions of human life are integrated.

However, what has been said about a recent approach does not allow of easy optimism. Because of long standing specialization and the segregation of the disciplines, many health professionals, as well as moralists, find it difficult to acquire a holistic vision and put it into practice. Alexander Mitscherlich surmises that an ignorance of psychology is "almost complete" among doctors.[10] The same author estimates that all somatic diseases are thoroughly or partially, in either their origin or their resistance to cure, psychosomatically conditioned. Moral theology and pastoral formation need to pay greater attention to this aspect.

4. Encouraging initiatives

During the last twenty-five years there have been many indications of a rethinking and of initiatives for new orientations in the whole field of healing, a turn to a holistic approach within the Churches and within the World Health Organization. There are hopeful initiatives of inter-disciplinary research by various groups. Worthy of mention is the ecumenical German Institute for Medical Missions in Tübingen in co-operation with a competent study-group of the World Council of Churches; the Kennedy Institute for Bioethics at Georgetown University; the Lutheran General Medical Center Foundation. A new creative model of holistic care for the terminally ill is the Hospice Movement, which originated in England and is spreading in the U.S.A. and other countries. Besides the classical forms of treatment there is special emphasis on a beneficent human milieu, an atmosphere of acceptance and loving care on all sides.[11]

3/1995

1 2 3 4 5 6 7 8 9 10 11 12 13 14 15 16 17 18 19 20 21 22 23 24 25 26 27 28 29 30 31

Time and again a holistic approach, including the spiritual dimension, leads to astonishing results in the care of the terminally or incurably ill where specialists in oncology and psychotherapists and logotherapists have worked together to create an aura of reconciliation. Thus, when the patient who has been declared incurable is reconciled with himself, his neighbour, with God, and reconciled also to his illness and the prospect of dying, the results are sometimes surprising. Life can receive a new chance of triumphing.[12]

NOTES:

1. J. McGilvray, *l.c.*, 83f.
2. *l.c.*, 56.
3. E. Wynder and H. C. Sullivan, "Preventive Medicine and Religion: Opportunities and Obstacles", in: M. E. Marty and K. L. Vaux, *Health / Medicine and Faith Tradition*, Philadelphia 1982, p. 231f.
4. Cf. A. E. Bergin, "Psychotherapy and Religious Values", in: *Journal of Consulting and Clinical Psychology*, 48 (1980), pp. 95–105.
5. J. McGilvray, *l.c.*, p. 40.
6. Cf. World Council of Churches, *The Healing Church*, Geneva 1966. Probably the best book on this topic is written by the doctor, psychotherapist and theologian, R. A. Lambourne, *Community, Church and Healing*, London 1963.
7. J. Murray Cudily, *The Ordeal of Civility*: Freud, Marx, Levi-Strauss, and the Jewish Struggle with Modernity, New York 1974, p. 10.
8. D. O. Foster, "Religion and Medicine: The Physician's Perspective", in M. E. Marty and K. L. Vaux (eds.), *l.c.*, p. 262.
9. M. E. Marty, "Tradition and Traditions in Health/Medicine and Religion", *l.c.*, pp. 3–26, quote p. 22.
10. A. Mitscherlich, *Krankheit als Konflickt* – Studien zur Psychosomatischen Medizin. Frankfurt 1975, 6th ed., vol. II, p. 7.
11. Cf. Sandol Stoddard, *The Hospice Movement*: A Better Way of Caring for the Dying, New York 1977; Rosemary and Victor Zorza, *A Way to Die: Living to the End*, New York 1980. (The last book is a moving story told by parents.)
12. Cf. O. C. Simonton, S. Matthew-Simonton, J. Creighton, *Getting Well Again*. A Step-by-Step Self-Help Guide for Overcoming Cancer, for Patients and Their Families, Los Angeles 1978.

Among the numerous publications on an integrated approach to healing, the following seem worthy of mention: World Council of Churches, *The Healing Church*: The Tübingen Consultation, Geneva, 1965; M. T. Kelsey, *Healing and Christianity In Ancient Thought and Modern Times*, New York 1973; H. Kruger, *Other Healers: A Guide to Alternative Medicine*, Indianapolis, 1974; G. Parkhurst, *Healing the Whole Person*, New York 1968; J. A. Sanford, *Healing and Wholeness*, New York 1977; Th. Sasz, *The Theology of Medicine: The Political-Philosophical Foundations of Medical Ethics*, Baton Rouge 1977; K. Vaux, *This Mortal Coil: The Meaning of Health and Disease*, New York 1978; H. L. Letterman (ed.), *Health and Healing: Ministry of the Church*, Chicago 1980.

CHAPTER TWO

CHRIST: THE GOOD SHEPHERD AND HEALER

Looking forward to the third millennium after Christ's coming, the Church needs, above all, to look to Christ as the Good Shepherd and Healer, and to commit herself to carrying out her mission to preach the Good News in an authentic image of Christ, the Good Shepherd and Divine Physician. The wounds to be healed are deep and terrifying. Will healing love be strong enough to encompass the healing power of our Saviour, Jesus Christ?

1. "I am going to look after my flock myself"

The image and role of Christ, Pastor and Healer, are portrayed beautifully and realistically in the prophet Ezekiel. "The Lord Yahweh says this: 'I am going to look after my flock myself and keep it in my view ... I myself will pasture my sheep, I myself will show them where to rest — it is the Lord Yahweh who speaks. I shall look for the lost one, bring back the stray, bandage the wounded and make the weak strong' " (Ezek 34:11–16).

It is in Jesus Christ that this text is fulfilled in all its truth. As he himself declares: "I am the Good Shepherd; the good shepherd lays down his life for the sheep ... I know my sheep, and my sheep know me" (Jn 10:11–14). In him, Yahweh — the "I am" — has drawn near to the sinner, the outcast, the sick, the downtrodden. He himself is our helper and healer. We can call upon him, entrust ourselves to him.

God does not meet us as a stranger to our misery, our illnesses and sufferings. He comes to us as the "One-of-us" (Son of Man), foretold by the prophet (Third Isaiah) and by prophetic events: "He proved himself their saviour in all their troubles. It was neither messenger nor angel but his presence that saved them" (Is 63:8–9).

Job, representing the outcast and untouchable, suffered most of all from the self-righteous judgment of the pious people who only came in order to look down on him and mark their distance from "that sinner". But what finally consoled him and put him on the road to healing was the faith-experience of God's compassionate presence with him. Job came to experience God as the compassionate One who is touched by his suffering. God assures those who trust in him: "I am with them when they are in trouble" (Ps 91:15).

Jesus, the Good Shepherd, takes upon himself the appalling suffering of the outcast whom those religious men who set themselves up as judges declare to be forsaken by God. Here we touch on one of the most characteristic dimensions of Christ's healing ministry: he heals the lepers by touching them, giving them the healing experience of human love and divine presence. Similarly, he rescues men and women who were social outcasts, scorned by those who did not feel their own need of healing and redemption. Jesus treats sinful women as persons, gives them back a sense of dignity. He does the same with the class of tax-gatherers and others despised as "bad characters", "hopeless cases". He eats with the friends of Levi-Matthew, the tax-gatherer, and even invites himself to the house of Zacchaeus, one of those who were looked upon as traitors and exploiters. Whoever, like Zacchaeus, gratefully accepts this rebirth to healthy and affirmative relationships, responds with a new heart, ready to convert himself, to make restitution and to give loving service to the poor.

Jesus, who in his divinity and divine mission came from heaven, heals by his warm humanity. His unlimited compassion has nothing of the condescension which, in human history, has so often hurt and even further degraded the outcast. By his closeness and total solidarity with the unclean, the poor, the sinner, he reveals the true image of God, Father of all. Luke, the physician, translates for the Hellenistic world the word of Jesus found in Matthew: "Be compassionate, as your Father is compassionate" (Lk 6:36). [The New English Bible comes close to this emphasis by translating Mt 5:48 as: "There must be no limit to your goodness, as your heavenly Father's goodness knows no bounds"]. The Stoic's God was considered "perfect" because he was unmoved by human misery — a God removed from sinful and passionate man!

The Japanese author Kitamuri is on solid biblical ground when he speaks of "God's pains" — God being deeply moved by our suffering and misery. Moltmann, in terms of process-theology, speaks of "the crucified God". This is an approach quite different from an

Anselmian soteriology where Christ's suffering and forsakenness become necessary for the sake of a vindictive, reparative justice on God's part. A theology and Church praxis which give primary importance to judgment and punitive justice, and in turn points to the sinner as an outcast, is far removed from Jesus, our Saviour and Healer, who is the only authentic image of God.

The kind of Church to be hoped for in the coming millennium is not a Church standing aloof in judgment but one which judges and heals conscious of being itself a "wounded healer", seeking to become ever more explicitly a sacrament, a true image of God's compassionate, healing love as revealed in Jesus Christ.

Our Saviour's redemptive solidarity with us will prove to be an indispensable criterion for the Church's effective presence in the world. He thus shows us the Father: "Ours were the sufferings he bore, ours the sorrows he carried ... We had all gone astray like sheep, each taking his own way, and Yahweh burdened him with the sins of all of us" (Is 53:4–6). That is Jesus' mission, entrusted to him by the compassionate Father.

2. Our Saviour: the living Gospel and the Healer

One of the most urgent tasks of the Church is to restore in her ministry and witness the synthesis between proclaiming the Good News and the healing of the sick which marked Christ's mission and witness. In Mark's gospel Jesus declares from the very outset that he has come to proclaim the Good News (Mk 1:38). Then follows the description of how he carried out this mission. While sharing the Good News, indeed sharing himself, Jesus casts out evil spirits, heals the sick, reintegrates the lepers into human society. Far from there being any dichotomy between healing and preaching the Gospel of salvation, it is while healing the sick that he announces that the kingdom of God has come. Healing and preaching the Gospel are jointly the way itself of sharing the Good News. It is in the act of forgiving sins, healing from the unrelenting leprosy of sin, that he makes the crippled walk again (Mk 2:1–12; Mt 9:2).

To the disciples of John the Baptist Jesus explains that what they had seen and heard — the healings *and* the evangelization of the poor — are the sign that he is, indeed, the Messiah, the sign of the coming of God's kingdom (Lk 7:20–22; Mt 11:2–6). In Luke's gospel in particular the healing power of Jesus is not completely accepted and accounted for until those who have been healed and all who have witnessed it give glory to God, rendering thanks and telling the Good News to everyone.

Many learned books and articles have been published regarding the miracles of Jesus. Some of their conclusions are relevant to our quest. The biblical accounts of Jesus' healing activity differ greatly from the legends of pagan religions about their miracle-workers. These latter stories are exotic, playing to the gallery, while Jesus severely rejects the devil's attempt to seduce him to perform miracles of a purely sensational kind. He equally rebukes the Pharisees and others who came "to test him, asking him to show them a sign from heaven" (Mt 16:1).

Certainly the healing done by Jesus is an unmistakable proof of his divine mission and power, but his healing miracles are, above all, signs of his divine-human love, a revelation of his compassion. And compassion provides not only a motive for taking action but also a medium of communication that energizes a person's own hidden resources. Even the evangelists' choice of vocabulary is significant. They intentionally avoid expressions which emphasize the spectacular, such as *taumasia* (stupendous events) or *teras* (extraordinary miracle) and prefer expressions like *ergon* (a work of deep meaning), *dynamis* (a mighty deed, energy), and *semeion* (a sign).

By healing, Jesus reveals himself as a friend of the sick and suffering. The way he meets people — giving them credit, awakening trust and hope, restoring in them a sense of dignity and personal worth — has a wonderfully healing effect on their spiritual, psychosomatic, and indirectly on the somatic well-being. The sick and the sinners do not feel condemned or judged, but loved, healed and forgiven (cf. Jn 3:17; 12:47). There is a deep significance in Jesus' declaration: "It is not the healthy that need a doctor but the sick; I have not come to invite virtuous people, but to call sinners to conversion" (Lk 5:31). It is a call to turn to him with trust and to receive a change of heart. Those who think they are in no need of conversion will fail to heed their Saviour and Healer.

Christ, the living Gospel of salvation, did not do away with all suffering, did not dispense us from dying physically, but he deeply changed the meaning and experience of suffering and death. By accepting the grace and instruction of our Redeemer, we shall be spared many kinds of illness and suffering and freed from a meaningless, frightening death. United with Christ we shall know that: "In Christ Jesus the life-giving law of the Spirit has set you free from the law of sin and death" (Rom 8:2). In a saving communion with Christ and rooted in the community of salvation, we shall be able to live in healthy and healing relationships with God, with our neighbour, our community and with ourselves. We shall heal what can be healed and be enabled to give meaning to what cannot be healed.

In many ways the Bible illustrates the profound relation between salvation and health. One aspect of this is that healing is an essential part of the proclamation of the Good News. It is an effective sign foretelling the final victory over the reign of the Evil One, a victory that will be most visible in Jesus' death on a cross, "so that through death he might break the power of him who had death at his command, that is, the devil; and might liberate those who, through fear of death, had all their lifetime been in servitude" (Heb 2:14–15).

For those alienated and locked into the solidarity of sinfulness, the Evil One — or sin-solidarity itself — in many ways has at its command sickness, suffering and death. But in a perspective of full redemption through the death and resurrection of Christ, the very fact of healing the sick and resuscitating from death — as in Lazarus' case — means that the final victory over sickness and death is announced. Further, for those united with him, Christ takes away from suffering and death everything that involves the reign of evil (that adds to the power of the "solidarity of perdition"). Whoever, in absolute truth, unites his suffering and death with Christ is freed from Satan's reign.[1] The very suffering, together with healing, enters into the reign of salvation.

For the Church's ministry it is important to see that Christ did not just tell people how to give new meaning to suffering and illness, and did not comfort them only with the hope of heaven; rather, he did all this in the context of his healing love and power. Only by healing whatever can be healed can we — the Church — help people discover the meaning of suffering in saving solidarity with Christ and with the whole community of salvation. All our God-given charisms, all our faithfulness to the Gospel and to the *diakonia* of healing come into play in the proclamation of salvation in all its true richness.

Nothing except sin is excluded from redemption. Through the Incarnation, redemption in Christ, and the coming of the Holy Spirit, human nature is marvellously restored. If, through faith and faithfulness to grace, we become healthy members of Christ's body, we become by the same token a source of health for others. We discover in ourselves and help others to discover in themselves the spiritual resources, the "inner doctor". Believing in Christ as the redeemer of the whole human person, the whole of humanity and the whole world, we shall unite our energies to promote healthy inter-human relations, healthy life-styles, a wholesome public life and a balanced ecology.

3. Gospel and healing give rise to a saving crisis

Christ, opening his heart as the Living Gospel and Healing Love, and thus reaching out to the suffering and to sinners, calls us to enter the kingdom of love and saving justice. He himself in his own person is a call to conversion, to a radical and decisive commitment. In this way he provokes a deep crisis in the sinner's heart. The sinner is called and urged to make a clear decision. Those who have experienced the nearness of Emmanuel (God-with-us) and the power of his healing love, and have thereby begun to understand his Gospel and himself as the Living Gospel, are drawn by the prospect of healing which he holds out. But the decision has to be made to receive Christ not only or primarily as healer and liberator from suffering, but first and foremost as the bearer of salvation which, indeed, brings healing with it. The sick and sinful person is faced with an alternative, either to open himself to his Saviour and Healer by grateful faith or to imprison himself in his own misery, ungratefully refusing faith and missing salvation, longing as he does for health only in an all too narrow sense.

It is not by command nor by the bestowal of benefits that Jesus seeks to elicit faith from the sick person. He is himself the prototype of unlimited faith by which he accepts his mission from the Father, and in its fulfilment he suffers with the sufferers and bears the burden of the burdened. In his twofold yet unified mission to reveal to mankind the saving justice and healing compassion of the Father, he is wounded by the refusal of faith and love. He does not seek suffering, yet in the cry of the blind, the sick and the sinner, he hears the voice of the Father, even when he is nailed to the cross. And he, who has healed so many, continues on his cross to call them to salvation.

The call to salvation coming from Christ, the living Gospel and loving Healer, is essentially a call to *faith*, understood in its full meaning as total commitment and surrender to Christ. The way to faith is marked by crises, just as the way to being healed and becoming "whole" leads through creative crises. Otherwise, the healing powers will come to nothing.

Brought face to face with Christ, who is himself the Glad News and Healing Love, each person must decide whether he or she will respond with an authentic "Yes", an honest, sincere "Amen": that is, with living faith. If one who has experienced healing love locks himself up in his egotism, seeking only earthly well-being, he as good as refuses the offer of healing and saving love. By separating health from salvation he falls short not only of salvation but also of the best of all healing and wholeness. He also deprives those around him of the witness of faith and gratitude. Therefore, Jesus cannot tell him, "Your faith has saved you", as he could the one leper who returned to him to thank him and to praise God by spreading the Good News everywhere.

Wherever Jesus heals sick people, not only those who directly experience his healing love and power but also all those who witness this event of God's nearness and power or who hear of it, are called to a decision of faith: to salvation. They, too, have to go through a crisis. Just as in Christ salvation and healing form an indivisible twofold offer, so the faith-response should not be to either health alone or to transcendental salvation alone. Christ calls for an integrated response in openness to salvation *and* health, loving adoration of God, healthy personal relationships and entrance into the kingdom of God — which is also a kingdom of saving justice and healing love.

Both the sick person to whom Christ has offered salvation, forgiveness and, at the same time, healing, and those who have experienced the nearness of Emmanuel take a great risk when they refuse this integrated response. By aborting the creative crisis they distance themselves still more from salvation and from the joy of faith, and are more than ever affected by unhealthy relationships and enmeshed in the unsavoury powers of the world around them.

It is true that Christ did not come to judge but to save and to heal, but it is also true that the way people respond to his coming and his healing nearness "lays bare their secret thoughts" (Lk 2:25). Some are thereby saved by faith; others pass judgment on themselves by their own refusal of faith.

The same is true for the Church's mission. Wherever those sent by Christ to proclaim the Good News and to heal the sick radiate both the joy of the Gospel and healing love and *diakonia*, people are effectively called to faith, to salvation in all its dimensions, including a higher level of wholeness, healthier personal and social relationships, a healthier life-style and a more wholesome form of public life.

By its inner dynamics, the crisis through which people go is meant to be creative; yet it can be abortive if they want to separate salvation from healthy human inter-relations, if they want the hope of heaven but not their personal share of responsibility for justice and peace on earth or, conversely, if they want earthly well-being but not conversion to the God of love and peace.

4. Christ our Redeemer

In a distinctive Catholic spirituality, faith in redemption calls for thanksgiving not only for redemption but also for the mystery of creation. God loves everything that he has created. Even after the Fall the human person remains marked by the fact that God has created us to his own image and likeness. The mystery of the incarnation, death and resurrection of Christ proclaims forever that God loves what he has created, and what was fallen and wounded is even more wonderfully re-created.

Nothing is excluded from redemption except sin, stubborn resistance to the Redeemer and to the grace of the Holy Spirit. The redeemed person can discover wonderful resources within himself or herself. Christ shows us how these resources can be awakened and strengthened. As Redeemer and Healer, he calls for co-operation and, above all, for faith which is the joyous and grateful acceptance of his saving and healing love. If we allow Christ to set us free for himself and his heavenly Father we can, in creative liberty, become co-workers in his mission of redemption. We can become healthy and healing members of his body. We can become a light for the world.

Paul, the apostle who has experienced the healing and renewing power of the Redeemer who rescued him from self-righteousness, feels how the whole creation eagerly expects a share in the liberty of the children of God (Rom 8:19–23). We still suffer from temptations that arise from within and are reinforced by the world around us. We are in danger of being wounded by other people's frustrations; we suffer and are sickened because of unhealthy relationships and unjust structures. But meeting Christ, the Redeemer, in grateful and trustful faith, we come to graps our mission to share the Good News of Redemption by healing people, by helping them to discover their hidden resources and to open themselves up to the work of the Spirit who renews our hearts and the face of the world.

We see how the world around us is partially enslaved by ideologies and idols, by consumerism, greed, sex-exploitation and many other forms of destructive behaviour, as well as by structural sins which spread unhealthiness in many ways. If we believe the Gospel of redemption, we can join our forces and our witness of love, as individuals and as faith-filled communities, in order to contribute greatly to healing many wounds: wounded hearts, wounded memories, wounded relationships. We can give witness of wholesome opinions and a healthy life-style. We can promote world-wide justice, healing and peace.

If we Christians would join hands and pool our talents, we surely could free humanity in a very short time from the plague of leprosy which still distresses more than 25 million people. And while doing this by small but specific sacrifices — refraining from smoking and other damaging habits — we could mark a beginning towards healing more and more facets of our sickly society and culture.

The first condition for all this is knowing Christ, the Redeemer and Healer, rendering thanks for the gift of Redemption, building up communities imbued with faith, and accepting our mission as healers of the sicks, friends and helpers of the needy, the lonely and aged.

In our Creed we honour Christ as Redeemer of the world. We honour him in truth when together we care for the wholesomeness of public opinion, legislation, politics and ecology of the world. As Christians, we learn from the gospels that healing has to rise from our hearts by a total turning to Christ and his reign of love.

5. Christ: the Reconciler, our Peace

Christ, our Redeemer and Reconciler, came into a world full of hatred, resentment, unforgiveness, anger and war. Because human relations were so deplorable, people made each other's lives ever more distressful. Into this world Christ brings the message of the Father that he is a compassionate, merciful Father, willing to reconcile all to himself and among themselves. And Christ gave the supreme manifestation and proof of this reconciling love on the cross: "Father, forgive!"

Christ's own compassionate and healing love, together with his Good News that conversion, forgiveness and peace are possible, make us sinners deeply aware that we are in need of divine forgiveness. From this awareness comes a new spirit, a new heart, with the total readiness to forgive our fellowmen just as the heavenly Father forgives and heals the wounds of our own sins.

Christ, the Healer, made two important points clear. First, none of us may look down on a sick or suffering person and consider him or her a greater sinner than ourselves ("we others"). We should learn from the Divine Physician to heal and not to judge. Second, Christ, by the very synthesis of healing and proclaiming the Good News that conversion is possible and urgent, teaches us effectively that unforgiven sins and unwillingness to forgive each other are the chief sources of misery, unhealthy personal relations and many kinds of sickness. He brings out the supremely intimate connection between actual healing and forgiving sins and leading people to forgive others wholeheartedly.

The gospel of Mark, which from the very first chapter gives prominence to the healing ministry of Christ, underlines this synthesis of forgiving sins and healing. Christ surprises everyone when he tells the paralytic man who is brought to him for healing: "My son, your sins are forgiven" (Mk 2:5). With word and sign Jesus explains the mysterious connection "Is it easier to say to this paralysed man, 'Your sins are forgiven', or to say, 'Stand up, take your bed, and walk'? But to convince you that the Son of Man has the right on earth to forgive sins" — he turned to the paralyzed man — "I say to you, 'stand up, take your bed, and go home' " (Mk 2:9–11).

This text and the whole manner in which Jesus combined healing and the proclamation of the Good News of conversion and reconciliation raise complex theological and pastoral questions about the mission and power of the Church to forgive sins.

I wish to mention only the principal questions. Should not the Sacrament of Reconciliation be seen and practised in the broader context of healing forgiveness? May it not be that the experience of healing forgiveness in the life of the faithful and of the whole Church is a condition for the credibility of the Church's power to forgive sins? Should not the whole pastoral ministry and particularly the celebration of the Sacrament of Reconciliation be seen more coherently in their therapeutic dynamics? Should there not be a more convincing coherence between proclamation by word and sacrament and the whole practice of forgiveness and reconciliation for all sinners who come with goodwill? Should we not fear more the scandal of excluding people of goodwill from the full experience of forgiveness than the foreseeable reaction of people who are inclined to be scandalized when sinners, whose sins are different from theirs, are reconciled not on the basis of accomplishments in law but on the basis of divine graciousness and goodwill? Should we not all have a livelier realization, and bring others to that realization, that the unwillingness to practice healing forgiveness is the greatest obstacle to reconciliation, health and peace?

Immediately after the prophetic story of healing forgiveness and healing-by-forgiveness, Mark's gospel gives a report which characterizes in a unique way the prophetic and healing ministry of Christ. When Jesus invites Levi-Matthew, the tax-gatherer, to follow him in intimate fellowship, Levi-Matthew, thus honoured, comes to a surprising and illuminating conclusion. He prepares in his house a meal for Jesus, to which he invites his old tax-collector friends, and other such "bad characters". Following the "logic of the heart", he thinks, "I am no better than these others, and since Jesus calls me, he will surely accept them equally".

This prophetic messianic meal with Levi-Matthew and his set, who are now becoming Jesus' friends, is a scandal for all the self-righteous who do not realize how sick and how far away they are from the liberating and healing truth. Jesus tells them that he "did not come to invite virtuous people, but sinners"; but unless the self-righteous adherents to a sterile orthodoxy realize that they, too, are both sinners and sick people, they will never participate in the messianic meal and never understand the biblical virtues of humility, gentleness, non-violence, graciousness and healing compassion.

Ministers of the Sacrament of Reconciliation, as well as other believers, can be healers with Christ only to the extent that they follow the example of Levi-Matthew, understanding themselves as "wounded healers" in need of healing forgiveness, and being gradually healed from the temptation to act as self-righteous judges. A humility like that of the newly-converted Levi-Matthew allows us to enter the realm of liberating and healing truth; that is, to know and to make known Christ, the Reconciler and Healer.

After having stretched out his arms, opened his heart and prayed for us all — "Father forgive!" — Jesus sends his apostles to bring, through the power of Holy Spirit, the messianic peace and forgiveness of sins to all people (Jn 20:19-22). Those who, with abiding gratitude, accept forgiveness and peace from Christ become his accredited messengers and ministers of healing forgiveness, although in various forms and with a great diversity of charisms. But for all, there is the absolute condition that, with heart and mind and will and with all their attitudes and behaviour, they pray, ". . . and forgive us the wrong we have done, as we forgive those who have wronged us" (Mt 6:12).

We cannot grow in the joy of salvation, in spiritual and psychic health, and become effective signs of Christ the Healer unless we are constantly and gratefully aware that we live by God's saving justice and healing compassion, and unless we make this awareness an unconditional law for our own attitude towards others and towards our ministry of reconciliation. Without this grateful consciousness and fundamental option, we are unable to know Christ and to follow him. Therefore, we cannot fulfil the mission to proclaim the Good News and to heal the sick, a mission entrusted to all true believers. We are even useless in the quest for true orthodoxy, for "the unloving know nothing of God" (1 Jn 4:8).

The more we live by gratitude for the undeserved gift of forgiveness and peace, the closer we can come to the biblical virtues of vigilance, discernment, hope and gentleness. Thus we become reconcilers and peace-makers, heralds of the Good News, "Peace on earth to all men of goodwill".

There is a considerable amount of literature today on the many people who become sick and are a source of frustration for others because they nourish grudges and bitterness in their hearts. They are unable to cultivate healthy and healing relations with others and, more than any other group, are vulnerable to illnesses of a psychosomatic nature such as stress and heart attacks. On the other hand, full reconciliation with God, with one's neighbour and oneself, a gentleness and readiness for healing forgiveness all greatly increase the chances to overcome not only psychosomatic but even somatic illnesses.[2]

A "eucharistic memory", filled with praise for the wondrous deeds of God and thankfulness for all his gifts and all our experiences with gracious people, is an inexhaustible source of health and healing, and perhaps the best contribution to the work of peace at all levels. Christ, the Good Shepherd, the Healer, our Peace, has taught us this clearly and emphatically. We can only wonder why we are such poor learners in this field while learning so easily many less important facts.

The arms race, the nuclear threat, M.A.D. (mutually-assured destruction), the age-old tendency to bedevil opponents are spreading distrust, hatred, enmity, nuclear bombs of self-righteousness and lust for power. Whole nations are sick, anguished, bitter. Without a change of heart at all levels, diplomatic negotiations will not solve these awful problems. Their deadly wounds can be healed only by going to the roots of the evil and learning from Christ how to become peace-makers and healers.

The disciples of Christ should be the first to use the remedies offered us by our Redeemer: the biblical healing virtues. The great Mahatma Gandhi has described them in the biblical sense as *satyàgraha*: healing truth, the force of truth whose heart is love. Those who live by this truth make the opponents their partners in dialogue and in the search for the next possible step towards fuller justice, peace and truth-force. The *satyàgrahi* do not know enemies as people to be destroyed or dishonoured. They help their opponents to discover their own inner resources: indeed, to discover themselves as brothers of all, seeing their own and other people's well-being by justice, sharing, and by healing forgiveness, without any trace of condescension.

The *satyàgrahi* realize how much undeserved credit they have received and receive constantly from God. Thus they are able to credit their opponents with good qualities and intentions, letting them see that they are trusted thereby to make an effective contribution to a common search for justice, truth and peace. Non-violent resistance confronts, first of all, the basic evils: self-righteousness, hatred, contempt for others, war-mongering propaganda, lust for power and for victory over others, even to the demonic point of demanding "unconditional surrender".

Today the *satyàgraha* alternative, as a new spirit with new strategies, becomes a focal point of genuine evangelization, healing ministry and peace mission. The time is over when a split between the teaching of dogmatic truth on one hand and healing *diakonia* on the other can be considered tolerable. Without the biblical virtues of non-violence and peacefulness there can exist no genuine and effective evangelization and pastoral work. Lately I have met people who, through the witness of Pax Christi groups and the "gospel of peace and reconciliation", have become interested in Christ and have come to know and to love him.

The Church's impact in the next millennium will be measured by her ministry of healing justice, compassionate love, non-violence, and the degree to which she lives her mission to proclaim the Gospel of peace credibly in an indivisible synthesis of pastoral care and healing love. She can help humankind not only to survive but to survive with dignity and under healthier conditions if she lives and proclaims that joyous faith, that total faith-commitment and love, those biblical virtues which are bearers of healing power. She can be what she is meant to be increasingly — at all levels a sacrament, an effective and convincing sign of reconciliation and healing faith.

6. The Spirit sent by Christ: the giver of life

Modern Americans speak of "health delivery" and of "health

industry". Neither salvation nor truly human health can be bought and delivered; they are not products of either industry or ecclesiastical "administration", and certainly not of an uninspired formal "administration" of the sacraments.

Christ calls us to salvation and truly human health, inviting us to himself, offering us the experience of his nearness, his caring concern, his saving truth and healing love. The kind of healing that points to salvation has to arise from within. Christ, who calls us to intimate friendship — which is the most healing relationship — sends us his Spirit to awaken and enliven our "inner doctor", our own inner resources.

Trusting in Christ and in the life-giving Spirit, we can face the dark powers around us and the shades within us. Our Creator and Redeemer shares with us great energies, a deep longing for salvation, for integrity and truly human health of body, mind and spirit. It behoves the Church to help us to discover these resources and to show us how to make good use of them.

Carl Gustav Jung gives as a rule to the therapist: "The best we can do is to give the inner doctor, who dwells in each patient, a chance to become operative". In much higher way, this is the rule for the Church's pastoral care and healing ministry: to help the faithful to rely on God's grace and, in that trust, to discover their own inner resources. That means to believe in the Holy Spirit, the giver of life, and to live according to the law of the Spirit who gives us life in Christ Jesus (cf. Rom 8:2).

Just as we can stop relying on "health industry" and "health delivery" and take our own responsibility for health through a wholesome life-style and a sound human milieu, even more so should we give up seeking false securities and entrust ourselves to the Spirit. His law is written in our hearts and can be grasped by grateful people whose lives are marked by adoration of the Father, the Son and the Holy Spirit: adoration whose genuineness is tested by healing love.

Christ, our Good Shepherd and Healer, has promised us the Paraclete. The Church, professing her faith in the saving and healing power of the Holy Spirit, is a joyous Church, a singing Church. With the Apostle of the Gentiles, she dares to tell us by all her life and ministry: "You are no longer under law, but under the grace of God" (Rom 6:14).

This, of course, does not mean the abolition of the Decalogue. What is does mean is that the Church shows us, by word and example, the way of the Beatitudes and directs us to the supreme criteria chosen by those who let themselves be guided by the life-giving Spirit: "The harvest of the Spirit is love, joy, peace, patience, kindness, goodness, fidelity, gentleness and self-control . . . If the Spirit is our life, let the Spirit direct our course" (Gal 5:22–25). Those who trustfully live on this level and, with God's help, try to do so ever more faithfully are hope-inspiring signs of salvation, peace and health.

The world of today is in dire need of these healing believers who fulfil the mission entrusted to them by Christ and his prophecy: "These are the signs that will be associated with believers: in my name they will cast out evil spirits . . . they will lay their hands on the sick, who will recover" (Mk 16:17–18).

There are many evil spirits in our culture, our economic power, in politics and public opinion. There are many wounds crying out for healing. The world needs holy healers who recognize themselves humbly as "wounded healers" and put their trust in God.

NOTES:

1. Cf. D. Stanley SJ, "Salvation and Healing", in *The Way* 10 (1970), pp. 298–317.

2. Cf. O. C. Simonton and others, *Being Well Again*, Los Angeles 1978; C. Linn, *Healing Life's Hurts – Healing Memories through the Five Stages of Forgiveness*, New York 1978.

CHAPTER THREE

THE REVEALING-HEALING MISSION OF THE CHURCH: BIBLICAL VISION

If we are to understand the full mission of the Church, her true nature and purpose, we must always bear in mind that it is infinitely more than an external mandate and an external institution. Above all, it is a wonderful sharing in the very mystery of Christ and his mission from the Father.

The fulfilment of the sublime mission, to proclaim the Good News and to heal, requires an interior assimilation with Christ, the Revealer and Healer. The Church cannot know herself and her mission without lovingly knowing Christ, and she cannot know Christ without being attentive to his ways.

Christ accomplishes his mission to reveal and to help in a totally unexpected way. He brings to it a new kind of authority, the prophetic authority of the Servant, and this should characterize the Church. And he is at one and the same time Saviour and Healer because of his total readiness to fulfil his mission in extreme suffering and humiliation.[1]

1. Sharing in the redeeming and healing authority of the Servant-Messiah

One of the firmest foundations of the power and authority of Jesus as Revealer, Saviour and Healer, is his humble obedience to the Father and to the Holy Spirit, who came visibly upon him during his baptism in the Jordan. By the Holy Spirit he was consecrated and sent in perpetual solidarity of salvation with sick and sinful humankind. By the same Spirit Christ is driven into the desert and strengthened to fight victoriously against Satan's most insidious temptations. By his firm "No" to the temptation to seek and offer material security, his "No" to vanity and purely exhibitional religion, and his final "No" to any kind of power or authority linked with the "prince of this dark world" of power and violence, Jesus shows us how to remove the main obstacles from our participation in his revealing-healing mission. He paves the way for us to salvation and healing.

Empowered by the Holy Spirit, Jesus purposefully chooses a poverty of earthly means and, above all, the new kind of authority, manifesting the coming of God's reign and kingdom. It is the authority of the "Servant of God", servant of the poor, of the outcast, the sick and downtrodden, indeed, the servant of all. By this irrevocable decision Jesus drives out the evil spirits. He drives away Satan.

Under the influence of "the authorities and potentates of this dark world" (Eph 6:12), who poison the atmosphere of human existence, humankind is greatly disturbed in all its basic relationships by domineering styles of authority: arrogance, exploitation, oppression, manipulation and deception. If such authority is exercised in the name of religion, the damage to human relationships and human health, as well as to structures and authority itself, is even more severe.

The coming of the kingdom of God in the messianic era is particularly marked by a new healing kind of authority embodied in Jesus. Jesus knows that he is sent by the Father and consecrated by the Spirit to reveal and exercise the authority of the Healing Servant. The Gospel is most explicit on this point. The visible descending of the Spirit on Jesus during his baptism was there and then interpreted by the heavenly voice, "Thou art my Son, my Beloved" (Lk 3:22), clearly bringing to mind the great prophecy about the "Servant of God" (Is 42:1). It is to this truth that Jesus calls our attention when he spells out the purpose of his coming (Lk 4:18). And having done so, he immediately embarks on proclaiming the Good News and healing.

But what matters directly here is that Jesus teaches his apostles and disciples most emphatically that their mission to share in the proclamation of the Good News and the healing of the sick presupposes the same fundamental voluntary commitment to simplicity and humble service (Lk 9:3; 10:3ff). Their whole conduct should show that they are not ashamed of the firm purpose of the Son of Man to be and to act as the Servant.

When the seventy-two came back from their first preaching-and-healing journey and exultantly reported that even devils submitted to them, Jesus told them to rejoice, rather, "that your names are enrolled in heaven" (Lk 10:17-20). This calls for a totally new way of life according to the heavenly ground-plan as it became visible in Jesus himself. It becomes even more evident when he praises the Father for having revealed his mysteries only to the humble ones, who are conformed with him to whom the Father reveals himself completely (Lk 10:21-24). Invested with the same "servant-authority", the disciples can "see" and thus reveal and heal.

This instruction of the disciples and their introduction into the mystery of salvation and this new kind of authority take place on Jesus' journey towards Jerusalem where his final and supreme revelation of the authority of the Servant will be made on the cross.

Jesus' self-revelation as the Servant and the instruction he gave the disciples took place in the context of healing from blindness. The disciples, too, are still blind until they recognize the healing-revealing power of the Servant-authority, and willingly become servants with him. Thus assimilated to Jesus' humility, simplicity and poverty, and invested with the same authority, they become prophets, healers, and heralds of the Good News.

Jesus fulfils his healing-revealing mission in the service of the poor, the beggars and especially of those who recognize themselves as sinners in need of God's mercy. He makes himself one of the poor, one of those who have no power — having rebutted the old authority structures. He is One-of-us in all things except sin.

The messengers of salvation and the prophets of the New Covenant are, therefore, essentially called to become like beggars, the most humble servants, with no thought for material security or provisions, fully aware, too, that they are in need of redemption and healing. Only thus do they know they are invited to the messianic meal, and only thus are they wholly open for the healing power and authority of Jesus.

The truth that the poor receive salvation and liberation through the saving authority of the Servant-Messiah is in the forefront of Luke's gospel, while the healing of the sick becomes the distinctive sign of that basic change in the meaning and style of authority. Once we have understood that "salvation is destined only for beggars and sinners",[2] we can safely conclude that it is Christ's wish to impart salvation and healing through prophets and servants who are even humbler than those beggars, sinners and sufferers.

In this light, the biblical narrative about the disciples' striking inability to heal the epileptic (Lk 9:37-40) becomes very revealing. A deep-rooted perversity stands in their way. The disciples, including Peter, failed to accept that Christ's mission must be carried out by him as a most humble servant. In consequence, they do not see the need for self-denial and configuration with the Servant-Messiah. Therefore, Jesus exclaims with great pain: "What an unbelieving and perverse generation! How long shall I be with you and endure you all?" (Lk 9:41). The same kind of perversity reappears in reprehensible form during the Last Supper when "a jealous dispute broke out: who among them should rank highest?" Jesus teaches them by word and example "Here am I among you like a servant" (Lk 22:24-27).

If, in the light of Luke's gospel, we ask ourselves about the causes of the long-lasting crisis in the ministry of salvation and the healing service of the Church, we shall realize that we cannot possibly escape into mere talk about new strategies and tactics. The very first requirement must be our configuration with the Servant-Messiah and the authority of his humility. We must earnestly renounce and withstand that false authority-understanding which Satan dared to suggest to Jesus. It is one of the most shattering truths of the Gospel that Jesus, with identical words and wrath, rebuked Peter when he protested against his Master's being the Servant-Messiah: "Begone, Satan", "Away with you Satan" (Mt 4:10; 16:23).

2. Sharing in the redeeming suffering and healing power of Christ

When healing the sick and proclaiming the Good News, Jesus, in a deep mystical sense, is constantly on the road to Jerusalem, on the way to the cross, knowing that the scandalous history of the murder of the prophets in Jerusalem will be re-enacted in him (cf. Mt 23:33-39). His passion, death and resurrection become the inexhaustible fountain of redemption and healing love for all generations.

We cannot remember meaningfully the compassion with which Jesus evangelized the poor and healed the sick unless we realize that his compassion is part of his readiness to accept the bitter suffering of the final passion.

Jesus calls "blessed" his disciples who become humble — like a child — because, freed from all spiritual blindness, they will "see" what the Father reveals in him (Lk 10:21–24). But he also expects them to be able to radiate the joy of redemption when they share in his suffering and persecution (Mt 5:10–12). Thus they become healing witnesses configurated with his "blessed suffering" and his resurrection.

By his active compassion while revealing salvation and healing the suffering, the sick and sinners, Jesus shows us the true countenance of the Father. This revelation reaches its peak when on the cross he prays, "Abba, Father, forgive them!" and then entrusts his spirit to the Father. In his supreme suffering there was unsurpassable compassion.

From the gospel of Luke we learn that "modern disciples need the kind of training in suffering which Jesus provided for his followers. It was by way of sharing in the messianic sufferings that followers would apprehend the powerful presence of the new age in the redemptive activity of Jesus".[3] Through configuration with Jesus' compassion and sufferings, the sufferings of his disciples — especially the sufferings which they endure in their ministry — also become a source of healing power. Minear concludes "It was the therapeutic power of messianic suffering which distinguished exorcisms and cures in the New Testament from ancient Hellenistic wonder stories as well as from modern faith-healing by revivalist preachers".[4]

Only by entering fully into the mystery of salvation, by which the endurance of human weakness in union with Jesus' messianic suffering becomes a channel of God's power, can we conceive of the healing power bestowed by God on faithful disciples who follow Christ the Servant, the Suffering Messiah.

The radiating joy and peace of messengers of salvation, even in the midst of suffering and persecution, the constant praise by those who have been healed and by redeemed people who experience wholesome and healing relationships, all point to the mystery of the passion and resurrection of Christ. This is an overall theme of the Acts of the Apostles and the Letters of St Paul. Time and again it is reactivated in the lives of the saints who were and are totally dedicated to the ministry of salvation and have received the charism of healing in the broadest sense.

This biblical vision and the experience of the history of the saints present a great challenge to the whole Church. The people of God must know that they cannot fulfil the unified mission to be both witnesses of the Good News and healers unless they enter wholeheartedly into the luminous cloud of messianic humility and suffering. Let us remind ourselves again that we are faced not with an imperative imposed from without but with the innermost sharing in the mystery of Christ who is the living Gospel and the divine-human Physician.

NOTES:

1. In this section I am particularly indebted to P. S. Minear, *To Heal and to Reveal: The Prophetic Vocation According to Luke*, New York 1976.
2. J. Jeremias, *New Testament Theology*, London 1971, I, p. 116.
3. P. S. Minear, *l.c.*, p. 121.
4. *l.c.*, p. 75.

CHAPTER FOUR

THE CHURCH'S MISSION TO HEAL IN TODAY'S WORLD

Before I wrote these pages, I consulted two new and much spoken-of books, hoping to find in them some insights on my theme: Franz Josef van Beeck SJ, *Christ Proclaimed* (New York 1979) and Johann Auer, *Die Kirche — Das Allgemeine Heilssakrament* [The Church: All-embracing Sacrament of Salvation] (Regensburg 1983). The very titles enticed me to seek there reflections on this theme. But my hopes were completely disappointed. The first book pays no attention to the healing activity of Christ as part of his revealing love, and the second fails to face up to the Church's mission to heal as part of the mystery of salvation.

I am afraid that this situation is indicative of a widespread omission, revealing grave shortcomings in both soteriology and Christology. Christ, the Saviour, cannot be faithfully proclaimed and the Church cannot be really understood and made visible if her mission to heal, as an integrating aspect of her mission as sacrament of salvation, is ignored.

The point to be stressed is the indissoluble unity of healing and revealing, of proclaiming, witnessing, celebrating salvation and healing. If these dimensions are severed, a kind of divorce takes place and both "partners" — the ministry for salvation and the *diakonia* of healing — suffer equally.

Since we look to creative fidelity for the here-and-now, the Church will first of all ask: What are the most pressing needs of today's world, of men and women of our time, in view of salvation and healing? Then follows the fundamental question: How can the Church, in faithfulness to her identity and integral mission, respond to these needs in full awareness of the intimate inter-relation between salvation, wholeness and truly human health?

1. Proclaiming and making visible salvation in its fullness

The Church has the mission *to be* and to become ever more visibly and effectively a sacrament, *"a visible, efficacious sign"* of salvation in its integrity, in all its dimensions. Words alone do not make the Church's sacramentality; all her being, all her dynamics, her countenance, her total witness, prayer-life and celebrations, together with her preaching and teaching are called for. And this means also being geared to the full concept and reality of salvation.

In an era of Cartesian dualism we spoke easily of "pastors of souls", thinking only or one-sidedly of "souls" and salvation in heaven. Today there is a strong and sometimes equally one-sided reaction against this verticalism and dualism. Some seem to see only the horizontal dimension of human well-being and justice.

Against this new trend it has to be emphasized that salvation comes from God and leads to God and his everlasting kingdom. This is the primary goal to be sought; then all the rest will come too. This, of course, does not at all belittle the commitment to justice and peace or to the wholeness of the human being, healthy relationships, integrity and health. All this can come truly only when deeply rooted in the whole of the reality and message of the kingdom of God. Setting priorities must not mean indulging in dichotomy.

The vitality of the Church in her human-social appearance and even in the fulfilment of her supreme ministry of salvation depends to a certain degree on the health of the society and culture within which the people of God live: the healthiness of the life-style, public opinion, public life and family life. Therefore, it is an integral part of the Church's salvific mission that she should care for healthy and healing human relationships at all levels. People's health, their capacity to open themselves to all dimensions of the messianic peace and to commit themselves to spreading the Gospel of peace and salvation have much to do with the Church's ministry of salvation and its integration of revealing and healing.

The dichotomy between verticalism and horizontalism, which today tends to split the Church, cannot be overcome unless pastors and faithful recognize that salvation, in its fullness, includes care for the *wholeness and health of persons* and of *public life*. All have to see that they cannot affirm salvation gratefully without becoming healthier from within and helping each other to find the full meaning of life, health and salvation.

2. The Church as reconciled and reconciling-healing community

The Church is a community of salvation and a healing-saving sacrament of reconciliation, coming from the Lord as an undeserved gift and a continuing mission and task for the people of God. For this she can attain inner health and unity only in reconciled diversity. The more she appreciates and sets free the diversity of charisms and the wealth of the diverse cultures and traditions, the more she becomes the health-giving and saving sacrament she is meant to be.

The healing mission entrusted by Christ to the Church is not something she can simply turn over to a chosen professional group or institution. She, herself, has to be and to become ever more a healing force as community of salvation and of healthy, saving relationships.

Let us mention just one historical example which can be discussed frankly today, since there is a turn for the better. If the Latin Western Church, claiming universal jurisdiction, makes or intends to make the Latin language and Latin culture the rule of conduct and criterion, she not only hurts and alienates other cultures but makes Latin culture itself less healthy, more arrogant and poorer. The Church herself becomes sick, tending to imprison the mystery of God and salvation in culturally too-narrow categories, thereby greatly diminishing her kerygmatic capacity and the necessary discernment between the substance of revelation and time-and-place-bound terminologies, symbols and structures. In this way the Church would greatly obscure and even betray her mission to reconcile cultures and nations and to lead them to an enriching and reconciling dialogue. She would greatly jeopardize her total peace mission.

Consistent fidelity to the doctrine that, before God, there is no difference between Jew, Greek and barbarian is part and parcel of the "sound doctrine" of which the Pastoral Letters speak so insistently (1 Tim 1 : 3f; 4 : 3; 4 : 6; 6 : 3; 2 Tim 4 : 3; Tit 1 : 13; 1 : 9; 2 : 2). For the author of the Pastoral Letters, nothing is more damaging to the community of the faithful than intolerant quarrels about man-made traditions, taboos and prohibitions. "Adjure them before God to stop disputing about mere words; it is no good, and is the ruin of those who listen" (2 Tim 2 : 14). Anyone who does not "give his mind to wholesome religious teaching, I call him ignoramus. He is morbidly keen on mere verbal questions and quibbles" (1 Tim 6 : 3–4).

In order to be a healing force, a faith-community should be deeply rooted in knowledge of Jesus and in wholesome doctrine and invigorated by healthy and healing intercommunal relationships and practices, including keen appreciation of special charisms of healing. But the basic healing activity is continuous and patient reconciliation within the community and through the community to a larger context. A reconciled and reconciling community will be ever attentive to maintain committed solidarity for the healing of the sick and for loving care.

Good Catholic teaching has always emphasized the uniqueness of each person. To cripple or oppress this uniqueness is to afflict both those who impose such deviations and those exposed to them. But it is equally true that individual persons cannot reach their own full identity and integration without realizing and affirming their rootedness in the community by active co-responsibility. Anyone who establishes the equilibrium between uniqueness and solidarity is truly a healing and reconciling agent.

The sick person is part of his family, kinship and environment. His chances for physical, psychic and spiritual health depend to a great extent on the spirit of responsibility and co-operation on all sides, including the sick person who should never consider himself or herself as a mere recipient, dependent on others.

A community that has a deep understanding of the salvific value of redeemed suffering — a redeemed way of dealing with sickness — can not only assist the sick more effectively but will also benefit from the example and prayer of those who have accepted the challenge of sickness.

We cannot cope with suffering in its naked reality. As such, it is not sent by God and can never be a source of joy or strength. But suffering, discovered as the redemptive expression of love and transfigured by the love of Christ, becomes the strongest expression of human solidarity, within the mysterious solidarity of God — through Christ — with us. When the Apostle of the Gentiles made this discovery, he exulted : "It is now my bliss to suffer for you . . . to complete in my poor flesh the full tale of Christ's afflictions still to be endured, for the sake of his body which is the Church" (Col 1 : 24).

I have had several opportunities to see how believers make this same discovery and how deeply it changes their life and even their suffering. Here I give just one glimpse. Sometimes I celebrate the Eucharist in the room of our Brother Alphonsus, who has been bedridden for more than twenty years and is now unable to feed himself. One day, when he was in great pain, I suggested at the beginning of the Mass: "Imagine, now, Christ coming in person and asking you to make a choice: either you become healthy again and able to work for the community with all your well-known skill, in which case you would still reach heaven, but alone, or — the other choice — you continue to suffer, uniting all your pain with Christ's suffering, and then, at the hour of your death, Christ comes in his glory and shows you a great crowd of people who, through your faith, your suffering, your patience and cheerfulness, you have inspired and helped to reach salvation. What would be your choice made in full freedom?" Alphonsus' reply was immediate: "The latter!" I know that our Brother had long since made this choice, but reaffirming it changed his whole countenance and appeased to some extent his pain, which he then brought into the Eucharistic celebration.

The inspiration so often given by the sick is a precious gift to all. And the constant care of the sick, the regular and loving visits to them, the meaningful celebration of the Anointing of the sick, all promote the salvation, integrity and wholeness of the community itself.

R. A. Lambourne has given marked attention to this insight and has deepened its theological vision. He sees illness and healing from within the passion and resurrection of Christ. "A sick person is joined to the Body of Christ. He is joined to the fellowship of Christ, the fellowship of the Holy Spirit and the fellowship of the saints. He is joined to the fellowship of love — the fellowship of love which is to be found in the local Church, and which, embracing the suffering of its own members and the suffering in its neighbourhood, is to be a therapeutic community".[1]

The Church is meant to be a faithful image of Christ, whose whole redeeming presence and activity is therapeutic, liberating, healing. He shows us that those who seek themselves and their lives selfishly, staying as far away as possible from the suffering of others, lose their true self, waste their life. "Here, indeed, is a mystery proclaimed in the life of Christ. He who would be made whole must suffer as he joins the suffering of man in Christ."[2]

In his Apostolic Letter, "Salvifici Doloris", Pope John Paul II treats equally the two directions in which true believers approach the various forms of suffering. There are those who become followers of the Merciful Samaritan, Christ himself, by healing and caring, fighting injustice and healing individual and collective wounds. And there are those who are suffering and, in their own outstanding way, become merciful Samaritans by sharing in Christ's suffering in the same kind of loving solidarity with which Christ accepted his suffering.

The Pope emphasizes that the suffering of the disciples of Christ is not only redeemed but enters creatively into the history and dynamics of redemption. "By bringing redemption through suffering, Christ has elevated human suffering to the level of redemption... Therefore, in his suffering man can become a sharer of Christ's redeeming suffering" (Salvifici Doloris, no. 19). The believer does this by entering fully into the healing and saving love of Christ while accepting this great challenge and test in the fellowship of disciples. Hence, the Pope appeals to these sufferers: "We ask you who are weak to become a source of strength for the Church" (no. 31).

Christian community education, a deep and constant experience of the community of salvation in the liturgy, teaching, preaching and in the whole life of the Church as a community, provides a good foundation for healthy relations everywhere: for alerting one's awareness of one's responsibility for one's own health (always in view of the health of the whole Body of Christ) and for active co-responsibility in preventing illness and promoting the health of all, including the healing of public life.

From a therapeutic vision of redemption and salvation flows a very challenging concept and ideal about health and healing. This could be easily misunderstood if one were to look merely for casuistry about rights and duties. If the point of departure is "health delivery" or the material output of the healing profession, the definition of health would have to be more modest than that of the World Health Organization, which speaks of "a state of perfect physical, psychic and social well-being, and not only freedom from illness and ailment". But there is nothing to be said against the effort of this organization to widen the horizons and to promote an ideal that should spur on every effort to achieve proper provision for fostering health.

Our vision of health and wholeness is even more challenging. It includes especially the spiritual dimension, emphasizes healthy relationships and the constant need and effort of healing public life. By the same token, our point of departure and our whole approach are more realistic. We start by considering the undeniable fact of weakness and illness which will never be fully overcome. We call for solidarity in order to avoid what are in fact avoidable evils, sufferings and diseases and so concentrate on healing what can be healed.

But then follows a wide range of challenges. We must discover the deep meaning that can be given to suffering, especially that part of illness which resists our shared efforts at healing. The faith-community surely does not need to confine itself to discussions about the why and wherefore of sickness and evil, nor even on how to master suffering and sickness. But the shared effort of fighting sickness and suffering has to go hand-in-hand with discovering and giving meaning to what cannot be healed. It is my conviction that the realm of what can be healed will thereby be astonishingly enlarged, and what cannot be actually healed will be freed from its worse poison: meaninglessness and rebellion. The contant experience of compassion and loving care, and the appreciation of the meaning of the highest values involved are ongoing healing events.

In a fallen and redeemed world, a true and fully human understanding of health implies a high degree of readiness to sacrifice and to suffer in active compassion or in meaningful acceptance of suffering, while at the same time all appropriate efforts to heal and to prevent illness are made.

Our model is Christ. He did not seek suffering as such, or unnecessary suffering, but he accepted all the suffering needed for our redemption, bearing the burden of all of us. So, too, in the therapeutic activity of the Church and in her compassion and shared suffering for the sake of healing and salvation, there is a privileged place for encouraging in ourselves and others a patient and meaningful acceptance of suffering that cannot be healed. This is part of the commitment in solidarity to heal and to contend against evil conditions and illnesses, especially those caused by irresponsibility or any kind of abuse.

In the war against contagious diseases and in the difficult struggle against the great "pestilences" of our modern time, such as alcoholism, drug addiction and the many diseases arising from irresponsible life-styles, the Church can and must follow the example of Christ. He liberated the lepers and whole groups of people from degrading judgments and alienation. The Church must do everything in her power to set energies free for healing and rehabilitation while contending against a loveless lack of concern and a harmful mental attitude towards the various categories of sick people. It is essential to give constructive education in personal responsibility as a means of preventing as much suffering as possible. But care must be taken to avoid creating a mental attitude of disdain or prejudice towards the sick, regardless of whether they have themselves to blame or not. The Church's attitude is to be not that of a judge but always one of therapeutic, loving liberation.

Around leper colonies in Africa I saw that among the Bantu tribes, lepers go through exactly the same kind of psychic-social suffering as the lepers in Jesus' time. They are considered as being punished by God or by the spirits for their own faults. They are despised outcasts. But under the loving care of Sisters and their helpers, the patients suddenly experience themselves as living, loved and lovable people. They discover that they are persons in the full sense, a dignified part of the Body of Christ. But then, suddenly again, this affirmation comes to a shocking limit. When the lepers are cured they cannot return to their families because, just as in Israel of old and in many other cultures, leprosy dissolves their marriage just as death does. They are also not able — especially in their cultural context — to live as single persons. But if ex-lepers then marry each other, they are excluded from the sacraments. Compassionate pastors tell them: "Don't worry too much; Jesus loves you beyond the sacramental system". They weep with them in compassion and tell them: "I, too, do not quite understand the Church's law in this matter". Yet I heard others say: "Why should we give them the Eucharist? They live in sin. Law is law". It was consoling for me when I saw an African bishop react to those words, weeping like a child or, rather, like a mother who weeps for her child.

In the fight against leprosy, which from a medical point of view could be easily overcome, the realization has developed that in the struggle against this terrible disease the most important dimensions are social, cultural, psychological and, above all, religious-spiritual. In the promising approach of "community medicine", these dimensions are not neglected. The Church has to tell people, not only by word but by conduct and in many ways, that leprosy is not at all a divine punishment; that leprosy is what people have made of it and still make of it; that this epidemic will one day be only a humbling remembrance.

3. The search for life's final meaning: the Church's logotherapy

Logotherapy, as proposed and elaborated by Viktor Frankl and his school,[3] is a dimension of professional healing-activity which shows great affinity and analogy to pastoral healing and redeeming ministry. Many are beginning to share a basic insight of logotherapy, namely, that health has much to do with discovering the deep meaning of life, and giving meaning to life through creative activity, harmonious social relationships, and by finally giving meaning to suffering. Healing is brought about, above all, through the discovery and implentation of meaning in a fully human perspective.

One must be really blind not to see that the worst suffering is caused by an aimless outlook on life, one that has lost even the basic impulse to search for genuine meaning and refuses to enhance one's own life and that of others with authentic values. To give up the search for authentic values and meaning damages psychic and even somatic health; it destroys or makes impossible profound human relationships. A human being lapsing into insensitivity contaminates the whole environment in its spiritual-humanistic dimension. It also has a share in all modern forms of pollution, especially cultural pollution. A life without meaning spells imprisonment, enslavement, enmity to the freedom which Christ has obtained for us.

The special realm of search for meaning and implementing it is community: people who care for each other, mean much to each other, live the reciprocity of consciences and accept co-responsibility.

Loss of meaning or of search for meaning can arise from a lack of experience of community, of affirmation.

Many go to the doctor or therapist without being organically ill. They are unable to tell what is wrong with themselves. They feel alienated, lost, depressed, disoriented. Frequently, somatic symptoms show up also. Behind this phenomenon there is often the loss of a value centre, frustrating purposelessness, some diffused disappointment. They have no one who means anything much to them; they have lost self-esteem, feel unloved, unappreciated as persons, nobody wants to listen to them with sympathy. They feel socially dead. This sometimes explains suicides. The attempt at suicide is frequently a last desperate cry for loving attention.

Every practitioner should know about these aspects and be able to offer some help in terms of logotherapy, some stimulation to search for a meaning to life. In many cases, however, what is most clearly indicated is to refer the person to a logotherapist or to a pastor who is competent in these matters. Insofar as the existential vacuum — the loss of meaning and lack of a value centre — is due to social isolation and gravely disturbed human relations, all psychotherapeutic efforts will normally fail, unless the social context and community relationships are taken into consideration.[4]

In logotherapy, special effort should be made to lead to a sense of community, to integration into helpful groups and to personal inter-relations that can become wholesome and helpful in the search for meaning. Since doctor and patient join in the ongoing search for a deeper meaning of life, the patient soon becomes aware that he or she ought not only to seek and accept help through contact with a healing community and dependable persons, but should also in turn begin to support others and his community on this ongoing journey.

Very frequently in my experience, a psychotherapist has suggested at a certain point that the patient should see a priest to talk more explicitly on the spiritual dimension of the person's neurosis or to reach a higher point through the celebration of the Sacrament of Reconciliation and Healing. On such an occasion, if possible, the priest should draw the person's attention to a group or community which can give support.

From both a pastoral and a therapeutic point of view, to use pastoral counselling and private confession and at the same time totally neglect to enlist community spirit and community building is a dangerously one-sided approach. Personal confession together with communal celebration of Reconciliation and Healing should be constantly used to foster the reconciled and reconciling community. The proclamation of salvation in all its forms should be on the lookout for the many opportunities which, by shared faith and the word of God, become a grace-filled locus in the search for meaning by those who are unsettled and those threatened by loss of meaning and value centre.

The healing mission of the Church and the concerns of logotherapy are not adequately taken care of by those who speak only in general and somewhat abstract terms about ultimate meaning. The person must be helped to search for meaning and authentic values in an existential way, in the concrete context of his or her life. In this search, one who feels oppressed by the fragility and futility of one's life and is angry about faulty conditions, while not yet being able or perhaps not yet even trying to face one's mortality, needs more than theoretical responses. Encouragement and support are needed, in order to master the crises of suffering in a meaningful way.

Authentic help in the formation of a lively *conscience* is one of the most urgent ways to carry out Christ's mandate to heal people. Here much can be learned from the principles and experiences of logotherapy. A Christian approach to formation of conscience will give marked attention to the primacy of grace and to the experience of gratuity and gratitude over and above law. Badly placed imperatives should never conceal the "law of grace".

Frankl rightly alerts the logotherapist never to try to impose his own convictions from without, or in an authoritarian manner, on one who wants to set out on his or her own search for meaning. Imposition easily becomes fully-fledged manipulation which blocks people in their personal search for truth and meaning. Logotherapy encourages the partner to dare the journey of ongoing search for ever deeper meaning, in openness to the Thou and We, and ready to receive witness and light from people whose lives give evidence of fullness of meaning.

This implies that the pastoral counsellor as well as the secular logotherapist will clearly concede to his interlocutor the right to doubt and to spell out his doubts. Even in matters of faith and morality there is need of a healthy way to face doubts honestly instead of looking for easy security and assurances. Of course, we have to discern between doubts, as an intrinsic part of the search for truth and meaning, and superficial scepticism or frivolous doubts that arise often from refusal to put truth and meaning into practice. I feel strongly that we have to give greater respect and attention to healthy doubts in an honest search for life's meaning. Respectful dialogue is the opposite of indifferentism and far more fruitful for both parties than arrogance and intolerance.

The Second Vatican Council's declaration on religious liberty, if seen in this perspective, reveals better its eminent therapeutic scope and meaning. It means liberation for honest search for truth in the reciprocity of consciences, out of respect for the traveller on his ongoing journey towards more light.

For a therapeutic moral theology, the elucidation of value and meaning is an indispensable presupposition for the liberating and healing teaching about norms and laws. Similarly, sound pastoral praxis will never try to impose by threats or manipulation a law or an imperative which, here and now, cannot be honestly interiorized by the person in question. It is not a matter of theoretical ignorance but of an existential impossibility. This was one of the strong points in the pastoral theology of St Alphonsus Liguori.

We have to distinguish between the individual judgment of conscience and conscience as endowment. The judgment can be erroneous; conscience itself can become sick. Logotherapy works for the healing of a sick conscience. (a) A conscience is sick when it has lost its inner dynamics for earnest and honest search for what is true and good — search for meaning. The causes of this can be manifold. One might be that parents, pastors or other educators are simply out to ensure security and submission, thus blocking the thirst for meaning. (b) A conscience is sick when it binds itself to law without discerning the underlying values, without asking first for meaning. (c) A conscience is sick when, through long and unrepented unfaithfulness to better insight, it has gradually destroyed its inborn dynamic towards "doing the truth" or, more specifically, "doing truth in love". (d) A conscience is deadly sick when it lacks reverence or openness for the conscience of others — when it has lost the reciprocity of consciences. We act logotherapeutically and pastorally by discerning and unmasking the forms of sickness in the individual conscience so that we may patiently assist the person on the road to healing.

Specifically Christian, pastoral logotherapy leads the searcher-for-meaning to Christ, who is the *Logos* and Therapist, the Truth, the Life, the Way to truth and life.

Bernard Tyrrell speaks in this sense about "Christotherapy".[5] It is a respectful, gentle guide leading the conscience itself to open to Christ, the healing Light.[6] And it is the task of the whole community of salvation, and of each member according to his or her special charism, to point the way to Christ by healing love. Logotherapy, like Christotherapy, happens when the dynamics of faith-witness are experienced through solidarity and reciprocity of consciences. Thus the community becomes the organ of Christ.

Such a proclamation of salvation and logotherapeutic pastoral life also assume respectfully everything that is truly meaningful for the individual and community in non-Christian religions and alien cultures — for these, too, are seeds of the *Logos*.

Genuine Christotherapy is an ongoing process of conversion and growth in the context of communities which are constantly on the road of renewal, clearly directed towards Christ and his reign of love and peace, indeed, guided by Christ himself in ever deepening solidarity. Christotherapy needs the co-operation of the whole community: of pastors, charismatic loving people and last but not least professionally qualified logotherapists.

NOTES:

1. R. A. Lambourne, *Community, Church and Healing*, London 1963, p. 120.
2. *l.c.*, p. 72.
3. Cf. Viktor Frankl, *The Doctor of the Soul: From Psychotherapy to Logotherapy*, New York 1973; Id., *The Unconscious God*, Austin 1976; Id., *Man's Search for Meaning: An Introduction to Logotherapy*, Austin 1970; J. Fabry, *The Pursuit of Meaning*; Viktor Frankl, *Logotherapy and Life*, New York 1980; see also: R. May, *Man's Search for Meaning*, New York 1953. Authors like W. G. Allport, E. Erikson, E. Fromm, K. Horney, C. R. Rogers offer also many elements fitting into the broad vision of logotherapy. Cf. E. Lukas, *Von der Tiefen – und Höhenpsychologie: Logotherapie in der Beratungspraxis*, Freiburg 1983.

4. Cf. K. Menninger, *Whatever Became of Sin*, New York 1973, p. 217.
5. B. Tyrrell SJ, *Christotherapy*, New York 1975; *Christotherapy II*, New York 1982.
6. Cf. A. Stanford, *The Healing Light*, Plainfield 1978.

CHAPTER FIVE

FAITH THAT HEALS AND SETS US FREE

Through the community of salvation and especially through holy, charismatic members of the community, Christ, the Divine-human Healer, awakes the "inner physician" dwelling and working in us through faith. It is through faith that we open ourselves to the healing power of Christ.

In this context we speak of that faith which becomes part of our whole being, persuading us to configure ourselves with Christ, to make our fundamental option for him and to embrace "sound doctrine" which will light our way to "doing the truth in love" and knowing Christ and the Father ever better. This is the faith which we celebrate in the sacraments of faith and through which we entrust ourselves to God — a faith that bears fruit in love and justice, and articulates and manifests itself in many signs of salvation and peace. It comes to its full embodiment in all the virtues, especially in the eschatological virtues so greatly praised by the Bible.

1. The healing power of faith[1]

Several times Jesus speaks explicitly of the connection between his healing power and the faith of the people he heals. To the blind man who entreats him, "I want my sight back", Jesus replies, "Go, your faith has cured you" (Mk 10:52; cf. Mt 9:22; Lk 7:50). By faith one opens oneself to the saving and healing power that comes from God and touches the innermost being, as if a doctor were dwelling there.

In order to unfold its healing and saving power, faith must be "healthy", able to respond joyfully and wholeheartedly to the love with which Jesus — Emmanuel, "God-with-us" — meets us: able also to respond to "sound doctrine" that does not stray into sterile theory or "disputing about mere words" (cf. 2 Tim 2:14). The faith that heals us welcomes God's life-giving word as the greatest gift and as a call to give ourselves as a gift in heartfelt gratitude.

Faith has the power to free us from guilt and anguish and to fill us with trust in God's healing forgiveness. In order not to deprive ourselves of this power, we shall never harbour a false, narrow image of God as a revengeful judge. Christians know only one genuine image of God: Jesus Christ and, in union with him, those who are authentic images of Christ. In healing faith we adore and "know" intimately Christ, our Saviour, the Merciful Samaritan who has come not to condemn but to save and heal us.

A healing, saving faith does not mean that we are guiltless. Rather, this faith gives us the humble courage to confess our sins, to lay open our heart with all its wounds to the Divine Physician. "If we confess our sins, he is just, and may be trusted to forgive our sins and cleanse us from every kind of wrong" (1 Jn 1:9). "Even if our conscience condemns us, God is greater than our conscience and knows all" (1 Jn 3:20). We can experience fully the saving and healing power of faith only if, while confessing our sins, we praise God's saving justice and mercy and firmly believe the supreme truth that "God is love" for all who seek him with a sincere heart. This does not mean that our love has to be perfect already but, rather, that we recognize the need of further purification and conversion and keep striving towards it day by day, moment by moment. Thus the process of healing will yield its fruits.

A most precious fruit and sign of the ongoing healing process is one's inner peace and the capacity to radiate peace and serenity. Miraculous forces flow, then, from one's spiritual centre into the psychosomatic dimension, and healing becomes all-embracing and, at the same time, a sign of salvation.

It cannot be overemphasized that we do not attribute the healing power to a momentary, transitory feeling of faith but rather to the "virtue of faith", as classical theology called it: that faith by which we faithfully follow Christ, remain close to him and grow in knowledge and love of Jesus and the Father. So the process of faith is a continuing and concurrent event of both salvation and healing.

We can convey the same truth by the expression, "faith conversion". Through faith in God and Jesus Christ, we make a radical fundamental option which strives after and fosters a constant growth in depth, an "ongoing conversion", as the Church Fathers express it. Yet this fundamental option can be in great danger of coming to nothing unless it unfolds and inscribes itself ever more in our striving, yearning and thinking, as well as in our conduct.

Believers, who in peace and joy have experienced the saving and healing powers of faith, proclaim salvation and participate in the healing power of Christ in a way that leads their neighbour gently to Christ, the Healer. This happens constantly. Take, for instance, "Alcoholics Anonymous" who openly praise God for the healing he brings about, thus inspiring new hope and trust even in those who have been considered "hopeless cases". A modern therapist writes: "It was William James who observed that more alcoholics have been cured by religious conversion than by all the medicine in the world. For all the immense apparatus of modern psychiatry, I suspect the same observation would be true today".[2]

Bearing in mind the very substance of faith, its saving-healing power and our understanding of genuine human health, it must be reiterated that we are here speaking of faith in a faith-community, in salvation solidarity. It can hardly be hoped that a faith-conversion, however genuine it may at first be, can be maintained indefinitely and deepened without the support of a lively faith-community with its communal purpose of giving thanks for support received by striving to be ever more effectively a healing community.[3] Thus the believer, on his road to salvation and healing is freed from isolation and estrangement. He is enabled to sense ever more clearly the closeness of the Emmanuel — "God-with-us". It should never be forgotten that worship — a genuine prayer-life in a faith-community as well as personal prayer — is the breath of life of a saving and healing faith.

Theology, too, can fulfil its therapeutic function and dimension only when it has its roots in a prayerful faith-community. If it deteriorates into a merely intellectual exercise at the level of scientific endeavour, it will be more an obstacle than a help for the healing and saving power of faith.[4]

Christian faith cannot be thought of without adoration, whereby man gratefully recognizes God as the source and goal of his life and praises him for the gift of revelation and salvation. By adoration "in spirit and truth", humankind finds its wholeness and centre. Believers find their own true self, healed from deception and confusion. This is part of the process of salvation but equally of ongoing healing through faith. Liberated from idols and dangerous ideologies, the believer discovers the way of salvation and finds courage and strength to overcome destructive conduct and break off harmful relationships. Those "who worship the Father in spirit and truth, such worshippers whom the Father wants", shall draw water from "an inner spring always welling up for eternal life" (Jn 4:24; 4:14).

2. The healing power of trust in God

One deep and dangerous suffering, which psychotherapists and pastors meet frequently and which sometimes resists all efforts to heal it, is a diffused and oppressing *anguish*. It has deep and wide-ranging ramifications with devastating psychosomatic consequences and should be carefully distinguished from the fear one experiences when faced with a concrete danger. Sometimes it may result from a sense of aimlessness and the loss of value centre. But, most frequently, it arises from a false, menacing image of God, distorting the whole existential pattern of life. Today we speak of "anguish neurosis"; moralists, since the seventeenth century, spoke generally of "scrupulosity". The afflicted person is not just tormented by doubts about whether this or that is a sin or even a mortal sin — although this, too, may be part of the suffering; what is more characteristic is an all-pervading anguish about being guilty and deserving punishment, distress at being a failure in what life itself is about, in spite of all one's goodwill.

In the religious history of humankind, people have suffered terrible anguish from a sense of being pursued by a vengeful god, vengeful spirits or a cruel fate. The Apostle of the Gentiles depicts the torment of people who seek in vain for justice by "keeping the laws" and imposing all kinds of laws on others because they do not know or do not accept by faith the healing-saving justice brought through our Saviour from a compassionate God.

Not every feeling of anguish is of itself pathological. Heidegger describes human existence as the state of "being-destined-to-death", and this reflecting itself sometimes in a tortured feeling, especially if the thought of one's own mortality is stubbornly repressed. If, on the contrary, the person achieves the freedom to face his or her death in an enlightened and meaningful way, many energies for health and creativity can be realised through a genuine "reconciliation" with the prospect of death.

The therapist, and often the pastor, meets people troubled by deep anguish that sometimes breaks through in time of illness, when they experience insecurity and an abysmal threat to their existence. This anguish in adult years can be very much linked with negative childhood experiences of rejection, reactivated by a legalistic religion wherein "the law" matters more than people. This happens more easily to people who are endowed with a deep religiosity. They yearn to know the God of love but are often confronted with religious authorities who rigorously inculcate legal or ethical do's and dont's which make little or no sense to them and cannot be fulfilled without great risks to their basic human relationships.

In certain periods of my pastoral and theological activities I was flooded with letters and visits from people who found themselves at the edge of despair and rebellion for reasons such as these. Reading the Gospel against the background of similar experiences, I fully appreciate what Bernhard Hanssler writes: "The therapy against anguish which comes from Jesus is immeasurable in its psycho-hygienic dynamics. The study of history of religions and comparative study of religions give all evidence that Jesus, among all founders of religion, is unique also insofar as he has removed from religion the anguishing elements".[5]

As the Emmanuel, "God-with-us", Jesus heals tortured people by his loving nearness, by loving affirmation. In teaching us to call God his Father, with the same loving and trusting word which he used — "Abba" — he shows us the Father. Sinners and outcast people feel restored by him to dignity and confidence. And this should be seen as a basic rule for the Church to which Jesus has entrusted the continuation of his healing ministry.

If God allowed me to ask for one charisma, I would not hesitate to ask for the great, loving art of liberating anguished people from this terrible plague. I have no miraculous power. But what we can all do, each in his or her own field and mission, is to remain faithful to Jesus by preventing anguish from recurring as much as we can and by doing all in our power to heal people who are victims of it. Let us ban the torture that arises from unsound teaching and unhealthy pastoral praxis. Teachers at all levels of moral theology especially must constantly examine everything to see whether it conveys the liberating message of the "law of grace" and show the healing countenance of the Saviour.

Laws and moral demands must never be severed from the experience of divine goodness and loving care. Those norms, which in the complexity of life often lead to severe conflicts with other pressing values and norms, must not be imposed with undue intransigence. Here we should be willing to learn something from the use of *oikonomia* (the therapeutic application of norms and exceptions) of the Oriental Churches and our own best tradition of *epikeia* (the virtue of liberating discernment) which reaches its peak when it is tested by the question: "What kind of image of God are we conveying? Is it the image, the countenance of the loving Father which Jesus has shown us?"

Whenever Jesus told sick people that they were healed "by faith", it is evident that they had great trust and confidence in him and, through him, in the heavenly Father. It was Jesus who awakened and strengthened that trust. In his person and by his deeds he invited them to trust him and so be liberated from anguish and doubt. The sick experienced him as the fulfilment of God's promises and his assurance of even greater events of salvation, liberation and healing.

Believers are on the road to salvation and healing when they entrust themselves to the Lord whatever may happen, confident that God can turn everything to our good. This kind of trust was expressed by the last words written by Dietrich Bonhoeffer on the very morning of his execution.

> Sheltered wonderfully by powers of goodness,
> trustfully we await whatever may happen.
> God is with us at evening and morningtide,
> and surely on every new day.

The new relationship of the redeemed person with the Giver of life and of all good things leads to meaningful trust in personal relationships and becomes also a source of trust for others, a mirror image of trust in God. At the same time the "inner physician", dwelling and working in us, directs our attention to the Spirit who renews the earth and the heart of man.

Trust in Jesus gives an abiding hope and at the same time frees us from false hopes and misleading aspirations. The One who has carried our burden unto the cross and prepared healing for us through his own wounds helps us also, day by day, to accept our cross and make our own the mandate to bear each other's burdens. Entrusting ourselves to the Lord, we shall experience what he meant when he told us: "Come to me, all whose work is hard, whose load is heavy; and I will give you relief" (Mt 11:28). Unwavering trust and joy in the Lord give us ever renewed strength and help us to discover new fountains of health and healing in the depths of our being.

An ever-returning theme in the Acts of the Apostles and the Letters of St Paul is that the disciples of Christ and heralds of the Good News can bring consolation and encouragement to their fellow Christians even in the midst of trials and sufferings if they have entrusted themselves totally to the Lord. Whoever has suffered with Christ is all the more able and willing to make the sufferings of others, as it were, his own, through compassion and readiness to make whatever sacrifices are demanded of him by active, healing love. It is in this way that we can all co-operate to transform suffering and give it a new meaning, so as to heal what can be healed and bear the rest with Christian hope.

3. The healing power of redeemed love

Whoever makes his own ego his centre of concern is sick and becomes ever more so. And he spreads his sickness to others. But an outgoing love, coming from God and leading to God, creates meaning and builds reliable bridges. Redeemed and redeeming-healing love is the most precious fruit of faith. Jesus healed people, above all through his love. This love awakened faith and trust in him. Martin Deutinger, a great moral theologian of the last century, hit the nail on the head when he wrote, "Only love can do wonders".[6]

Redeemed and redeeming love can harness people's healing energies. It opens up the greatest treasure of meaning and purpose and indeed, all the riches of the kingdom of God. This love is at the heart of the proclamation of salvation, pointing and leading to the final celebration of love in the Communion of Saints, where salvation, beatitude and human wholeness will be brought together.

It is impossible to overrate the therapeutic power of redeemed love, for this is an essential dimension of salvation and redemption. We must, however, be quite clear that we are speaking about the right kind of love. For this indispensable discernment, Scripture gives us clear criteria in all that is said, for instance in 1 Corinthians 13 and Galatians 5, about Jesus' love, which is the source and model of redeeming love. We dare to add that, for us and for our witness, the healing power of personal relationships, the discovery of our own and others' inner healing resources and co-operation in view of healing public life are among the most striking and encouraging signs of genuine love.

"There is nothing love cannot face; there is no limit to its faith, its hope, and its endurance" (1 Cor 13:7). By gracing our hearts with his love, God gives us a tremendous and most precious reserve of help for others. This same love enables us to draw from that reserve to instil in them a foretaste of goodness and trust. And this very advance of trust can be itself a healing power.

4. The saving and healing power of the eschatological virtues

As we have seen, faith, hope and love manifest the saving and healing presence of the kingdom of God. They are signs of the "end of times". They give form and strength to all the other virtues.

In this context I do not intend to speak about the four "cardinal virtues" which the Church adopted and adapted from Hellenistic culture. For our purpose it is much more helpful and significant to give more consideration to those biblical virtues which, besides faith, hope and love and as a manifestation of them, insert the believer as an active participant into the history of salvation and thus also into the history of healing.

Since our prevailing interest here is insertion into the dynamics of the history of salvation, I place these biblical virtues according to the three dimensions of history: past, present and future.

a) *Gratitude*

With St Alphonsus, I consider *memory* as the most basic gift, without which the other powers such as intelligence and will are inconceivable. Memory makes us active participants in history. It allows the riches of the past to become operative in the present. It calls for and provides coherence and fidelity.

Through a *grateful* memory, all that God has done up to now, all the marvellous achievements of humankind in the past and all that is precious in tradition can be revitalized. The past is made present to us, ready to be turned to good account here and now. Our own inner value and strength depend to a great extent on a grateful memory. This biblical virtue enables us to celebrate meaningfully and live faithfully the Eucharist, which means "thanksgiving". A grateful memory makes us willing and able to share what we have received in the past and from the past. We not only draw lessons from it, but energize it, revitalize it and bring it to new fruition.

The importance of gratitude — understood as *grateful memory* — becomes more evident when we think of the opposite: a poor, sick memory occupied by resentments, grumblings, grudges, which impoverishes the individual and the community. Even worse, the sick memory is destructive. It reactivates the worst of the past in an unredeemed way. It constantly reopens, deepens and poisons old wounds and scars. The ungrateful have nothing to contribute to the present hour. They waste time in lamentation and accusation. They are discontent and, therefore, are not free to appreciate others or even themselves in a healthy way.

The grateful person is a gracious sharer, never condescending, for he knows that what he shares has been given to him and can remain a precious gift only when gratefully shared. Thankful people not only have open eyes for all the good they have inherited from the past; they also open the eyes of others, to free them gradually from their self-destructive grudges. One of the greatest achievements in healing is the healing of wounded memories. A community of grateful believers — a truly "Eucharistic community" — is a fountain of health and healing.

b) *The virtues of the present moment*

Gratitude is built up from its foundations by those biblical virtues which open the eyes of the believer to the present opportunities, the present moment (*kairos*), this hour of salvation (*hora*). The virtues that enable us to grasp the offering of the present moment are: *vigilance, readiness, discernment*. We cannot live healthily in the presence of the Lord of history without a keen appreciation of every moment that invites us to be co-actors in the history of salvation and healing.

In many parables and admonitions the Lord and the apostles show us the importance of *vigilance*: watchfulness for the Lord's coming. If we live in his presence, always ready to see what the present moment requires of us, our whole life becomes the prayer: "Lord, here I am, call me! Send me!" Thus we shall be prepared for his final coming when he will come to call us home at the hour of our death.

Readiness comes from the overflow of gratitude and vigilance. It is a sign of our conformity with the will of God, as well as a criterion for discernment. This attitude of readiness prevents us from indulging in star-gazing and day-dreaming and vagaries about what things may mean. We open ourselves to the gift of discernment, trying to discover the existential meaning of "this hour" in the service of the kingdom of God.

Discernment asks: "What, here and now, can be my acceptable contribution to the ongoing history of salvation, liberation and healing?" It is those who are open to all the dimensions of history who will find the best answers to such questions as what, here and now, is the best possible way of expressing my gratitude? What is the next step towards the future? What can I render to the Lord for what he has done for me? How can I serve those who are my companions on the journey of salvation history?

Desires, words and deeds that would deprive us of serenity and peace of mind cannot be the appropriate contribution to the here-and-now situation. Discernment sometimes requires that we first summon our inner peace. Then we can deal with grave problems and make daring decisions.

To understand better the healthy and healing quality of the

virtues of the present moment, we can look again at the opposite, to the barren people who seem to live constantly on the verge of "if only": "If only this or that were different, what wonders I could do!" Unhappy, estranged, they always miss the present hour.

c) *The dimension of the future and its virtues*

The Christian's future is illumined by hope based on the divine promises. Hope in the fullest sense offers a clear goal. The accompanying virtues are responsibility for the near future — a future of peace, justice, wholesome public life — and the responsibility of passing on to new generations a healthy social and ecological environment.

Eschatological hope allows our dreaming of *utopias*, probing for better models for a human future as, for instance, peace-making. These underlie discernment, where all the eschatological virtues play a role. We shall never work for utopias which betray the *presence* — the presence of the moment and the immediate presence of God and of people as the Marxist utopia does, besides contradicting the final hope of mankind.

If a sick person has helpers and friends stamped with these biblical virtues, he will be able to discover meanings to his circumstances, and bring to light his own inner powers and, above all, realize the positive opportunities that present themselves. Christian hope and all the other virtues are distinguished by the light and direction they give when we have to look for the meaning of suffering and disappointment.

The eschatological virtues imply that we are on the road with Christ who is the Way, the Truth and the Life. And, being his disciples, we are all united on this road in solidarity.

5. The healing energies of the sacraments of salvation

As we have seen, the biblical virtues insert us wholly and actively in the history of salvation and healing. But we should not forget for one moment that all this happens through grace. The sacraments of salvation are channels of God's saving and healing grace. They teach us and enable us to become both receptive and creative in the cause of salvation history.

Christ is the origin and centre of all the effective signs of salvation, the originating sign-sacrament. In him and through him the Church is to be ever increasingly an all-embracing, efficacious sign (sacrament). Her first mission is not "to do" but "to be" so that her authentic countenance — the saving-healing love of Christ — shines through her very being and becomes visible and accessible to faith-experience. The effectiveness of her saving-healing pedagogy depends on how much the Church as a whole, each Church community and each of her members become a kind of sacrament, an attractive, energizing sign of redeemed and redeeming, saving and healing love.

The seven sacraments of the Church and all the other signs and symbols of salvation are directed to the continuing event of salvation history. If we want to penetrate more deeply into the synthesis of proclamation-celebration of the mystery of salvation and the healing ministry, we must pay much attention to this vision of sacramentality and faith-witness. It is a saddening fact that, during past centuries, moral theology and catechisms dealt with the sacraments only *after* the commandments, and with a very legalistic casuistry. The result was, to a great extent, a sterilizing blindness to the healing power of the sacraments and of the Church at large.

a) *The saving-healing power of Baptism*

Bible, tradition and liturgy teach us to see Baptism as an event of new creation. The believer, through grace, faith and the effective signs of faith, is a new creation with new saving relationships with God, Father of all, with Christ, Saviour of all, and with the Holy Spirit who renews the face of the earth and the hearts of the people of God. As a consequence, there arise also new saving-healing, liberating relationships with all the redeemed, with the world redeemed by Christ, with culture, society and the earth itself. The more substantial these relationships are, the more fully will the baptized live the gift and mission bestowed on them in Baptism.

Since the sacraments insert us into the history of salvation, we do not think just about the actual moment of the reception of Baptism. Rather, we see the event of Baptism as an important point of departure, a divine assurance and the believer's commitment to live and to grow ever more truthfully in accordance with this sacrament of faith, salvation and healing.

b) *The sacrament of Confirmation*

Confirmation opens our heart and directs our attention to the "Spirit of truth" who, from within, teaches us genuine love, enables us to live a life of truth, leads us to authentic maturity, strengthens us on the road to full responsibility, and protects our psychic and spiritual life from all crippling selfishness, both individual and collective. As Christians we know that the "Spirit of truth" is the real source of *satyàgraha*, the strength of truth in us.

Confirmation signifies the abiding gift of strength which will enable us to embrace gratefully and courageously our mission and responsibility for the health of public life. Confirmed believers can and must be fully aware that their own salvation and wholeness-identity-integrity depend very much on how faithfully they carry out their commitment to the Saviour of the world. This entails responsibility to work, together with all people of goodwill, for wholesome public opinion, a more mature and balanced culture, economy and political life, so as to build a more just, more peaceful and healthier world.

c) *The saving-healing power of the Eucharist*

In Christ and in the Church, the Eucharist is the central and most fruitful sacrament of the saving-healing grace of God. It is also a principal sign of "forgiveness of sins", of healing hurt memories, a source of peace and an energizing resource for the peace-mission of all Christians. The Eucharist is an efficacious sign of healing faith, hope and love that enables the community and each believer to radiate wholeness and peace, to serve the poor, to care for the sick and to heal the depressed and the anguished. When rightly celebrated, it communicates that joy in the Lord which is a source of strength and health.

The Eucharist is a memorial celebration through which we meet Christ in grateful remembrance of how he reached out to the outcast and the sick while proclaiming the Good News. Through a grateful memory we live in the presence of Christ and experience, in faith, how he identified and still identifies himself with our sufferings and with a sick humanity. When, in this memorial, we praise him for having borne our burden, he inscribes in our hearts and memories his mandate to bear a part of the burden of others, especially of the sick. Thus, we participate in his caring-healing ministry.

Just as in Christ's earthly mission the proclamation of salvation was firmly united with his healing activity, so in the Eucharistic memorial the faith-experience of Jesus' sacrificial love cannot be severed from the call of the needy, suffering and sick, through whom Christ turns to us and tests our faith.

The saving word of Jesus in the Eucharist, "Do this in memory of me", reminds us gently but inexorably of the anticipated final judgment: "You have visited me when I was sick ... Whatever you have done to the least of my brethren, you have done to me". These two sayings urge us to take a clear decision both for Christ and for the suffering members of his Body. How could we truthfully say our "Amen" to the word, "This is my body", if we were to withhold our "Yes, here I am" when members of Christ's Body cry out in their suffering for love, care and help?

When we receive the body of Christ we are always confronted with his question as to whether we want to be truly at one and to act in solidarity as corporate members of the Body of Christ. A truly Eucharistic, grateful memory will help us to say our responsible "Amen" when the need of others appeals to us for our active love. The creative, healing, caring solidarity of the Christian community with the sick and suffering is an integral dimension of the Eucharistic memorial and of a faith-filled memory bearing fruit in caring, healing love.

The Eucharistic ministry by which Communion is brought to the aged, disabled and sick, is thoroughly consistent only to the extent that the whole Eucharistic community participates in caring-healing assistance and gives it according to the charisms and capacities of each and all of its members. However, we should not overlook another aspect: the sick and their families, who have their share in the suffering, are drawn into the two-fold invitation, Christ's bidding, "Do this in memory of me", and the appeal to be ever more increasingly active members of Christ's Body. Their creative suffering and the family's loving care can enter effectively into the total mission of the Church to reveal, to suffer and to heal. It is their true "Amen", renewed day by day, a continuing gift to the Body of Christ. For themselves and for others, this has a saving-healing power. Their suffering and caring, united with the Eucharistic-healing community, has a bearing on the salvation, wholeness and health of all.

No effort towards a faithful fulfilment of the two-fold yet unified mission to proclaim the Good News and to heal, to be lovingly present to the suffering, can ignore these dimensions of the Eucharist and a Eucharistic spirituality.[7]

d) *The sacraments of Healing, Forgiveness and Reconciliation*

In order to proclaim the Gospel and to heal, it is vitally important for the Church to see the sacraments, which are empowered to bring forth forgiveness of sins, in a clear relationship with her healing ministry. Here we face a clear ecumenical opportunity. If the Roman Catholic Church is humble enough to recognize the fact the Orthodox Churches have an important lesson to teach us. They have always seen the mystery of redemption as well as the sacraments of forgiveness, in the light of healing. I say the "sacraments" because, for Oriental Christians, just as for the Western (Latin) Church of ancient times, the Eucharist has always been seen as a *therapeutic* event of forgiveness of sins and the granting of peace: "This is the cup of my blood ... for the forgiveness of sins". The specific sacrament of Reconciliation (called in the West, "Penance" or "Confession") was seen explicitly as empowered by the Eucharist and directed towards it.

In the West the sacrament of Penance came to reflect the theory of redemption prevalent since the time of St Anselm, which saw it chiefly in terms of reparation demanded by vindictive justice. So Penance, and later the painful, accurate confession, conceived as punishment-reparation (receiving its merits from the reparation wrought by Christ), lost their emphasis on therapy. This thought-pattern was also a reflection of a vindictive justice pattern of contemporary culture. Meanwhile, in the Eastern Church the ordinary confession — as distinct from the rehabilitation processes after grave, criminal or gravely scandalous sins — was thoroughly understood in the light of Christ's words: "I have come to heal sinners".

It has to be noted, however, that even in the West the therapeutic emphasis has repeatedly found its supporters. Outstanding amongst them is St Alphonsus. With great courage he withstood the tide of current trends. In his book written for the general run of pastors he explains the ministry of the confessor. In the *first* place, he says, comes the ministry of a father, of one who, by his loving kindness and compassion, makes visible the heavenly Father. Every Christian, then, has to give prime attention to Jesus' word: "Be compassionate just as your heavenly Father" (Lk 6:36). In the *second* place, the confessor is to be a healer — image of Christ's mission as the Healer and sharer in it. This is possible only if the confessor helps people to experience the compassion of the heavenly Father. In the *third* place, the confessor is to be a "teacher of the law", the law of Christ, law of love and saving-healing solidarity. He is expected to teach "sound doctrine" in the sense of the Pastoral Letters quoted earlier in this book. He must never inculcate man-made traditions or doctrines to the detriment of the all-embracing vision of the love of God and of one's neighbour. Above all, the confessor must respect the penitent's sincere conscience even if he thinks he has good reasons to consider it erroneous. He may never manipulate anyone's conscience, but rather will help the person, in the light of Jesus, to search for what is true, good, beautiful and healing. In the *last* place of all comes mention of the ministry of judge.[8] Seen in the full light of the other main dimensions, the ministry of judge includes nothing that might threaten the penitent or provoke anguish. On the contrary, it means guiding each other towards the vision of God's saving justice, to a sense of discernment and to a readiness to make amends, especially when it is a matter of healing wounds inflicted on others or repairing as far as possible the damage done by scandal. This is often indispensable for the penitent's own healing, wholeness and genuineness.

My belief is that the present crisis of the sacrament of Penance could be overcome if it were better understood as sacrament of *Reconciliation and Peace* in this integrated vision. This applies as much to individual confession as to the communal celebration of the sacrament. The two forms do not compete but, rather, complete each other.

This understanding of the sacrament can also liberate people from an unhealthy obsession created by a simplistic distinction between "serious and venial sins" or "grave and only venial sins", whereby the words "serious" and "grave" mean, for many, the distinction between "mortal and 'merely' non-serious sins". Thus, a distinction becomes impossible in a therapeutic approach. Of course, "mortal sin" is most serious, just as meaningless death is. But no doctor would call death alone a "serious" or "grave" matter. He is faced with all conceivable degrees of gravity, and he knows that sometimes a lesser illness, if left untreated, can develop into grave, very serious, extremely serious, and finally deadly illness.

A Christian who has this therapeutic understanding of the sacrament will not tell himself, "My sins are not mortal; therefore, I don't need the sacramental encounter with Christ, the Healer". On the contrary, in honour of Christ the Healer and in his own interest, he will do his best, by earnest repentance, trust, serious endeavour and by the sacrament of Reconciliation and Peace, to prevent his spiritual illness from developing into a grave and finally mortal downfall.

e) *The sacrament of the healing Anointing of the sick*

The saving-healing dimension of the sacrament of Anointing the sick is particularly evident in both Scripture and considerable portions of the liturgical tradition. In the West for many centuries the term "Extreme Unction" has obscured the therapeutic dimension by frightening people and discouraging them from its timely reception. The Second Vatican Council has restored the emphasis on healing. "Extreme Unction, which may also and more fittingly be called 'Anointing of the sick', is not a sacrament only for those who are at the point of death. Hence, as soon as anyone of the faithful begins to be in danger of death from sickness or old age, the appropriate time for him to receive this sacrament has certainly already arrived".[9]

The biblical text frequently quoted in this context is even clearer regarding the synthesis of saving and healing power. "Is one of you ill? He should send for the elders of the congregation to pray over him and anoint him with oil in the name of the Lord. The prayer offered in faith will save the sick person, the Lord will raise him from the bed, and any sins he may have committed will be forgiven. Therefore, confess your sins to one another, and then you will be healed" (Jas 5:14–15).

The wording in the original Greek text reminds the reader even more of the relation between raising the sick from their bed and raising them to everlasting life, between healing and saving. This text, like the various liturgical rites, also emphasizes the community aspect of caring, healing, saving. It is heartening to see now, in so many places all over the world, loving and healing community celebrations of the sacrament of Anointing the sick, sometimes in connection with the Eucharistic celebration. The way in which the parish community co-operates, concelebrates and receives new inspiration for the care of the sick, the elderly and the lonely is not the least of the blessings of this creative return to one of our oldest traditions.

In the same light we rediscover the role of our senior citizens ("elders" in the broad sense). Many of them have learned to visit the sick and especially the lonely, combining acts of help with cheerful listening, conversation, comfort and prayer. In the Anointing of the sick, seen in connection with this meaningful visiting, a tri-unity of (1) healing love, (2) comforting faith and (3) redeeming-saving suffering can be brought about.

(1) The community of the faithful, through the sharing and caring of its members, aims at helping people to experience Christ's healing love for the sick. The heartfelt love for the person in question is fruit of faith in the redeeming, healing love of Jesus.

(2) The sick person is comforted and strengthened by the witness of faith which speaks not just in words but in the integrated truth of life, sharing and caring.

(3) Thus, the suffering of the sick person enters more fully into the light of Christ's suffering and healing. By discerning the deeper meaning of suffering, the "poison" is dissipated. Whatever can be healed will be healed, and the rest will be no longer meaningless, depressing suffering.

The sick are not just passive recipients. In accepting the sharing-caring love of others and their thoughtful witness of faith, they themselves become radiating, healing, saving centres of the tri-unity of love-faith-and-Christlike suffering. They are important partners in the saving-healing love and suffering of Christ, for the good of the whole Body of Christ.

The more the faith-community learns to understand this synthesis of love, faith-witness and suffering, the more effectively and generously can the sick receive and return it. Thus, the sick and their families are much more than objects of pastoral care; they are frequently able to give in return more than they receive, in wonderful reciprocity.

f) *The healing power of the sacrament of Matrimony*

A misdirected tradition has spoken of the healing aspect of Matrimony only in the narrow perspective of the doctrine of the goals of marital intercourse (healing and/or quietening concupiscence). The true vision is, of course, far more beautiful. Spouses, parents, children, all members of the family, are called and enabled to be for each other efficacious signs of God's saving-healing love, through their healthy and healing relationships. They should be fully conscious that they are, through grace, fellow-travellers on the road to maturity, wholeness, salvation, holiness.

Care must be taken that the engaged couple does not indulge in utopian dream-images. The betrothed should be sure to accept each other in their complex reality, with their inner qualities *and* with their shades and wounds to be healed. The more they help each other in grateful, mutual acceptance to discover their inner resources the better they can deal with their shades.

For all the members of a Christian family Viktor Frankl's expression is particularly meaningful: "Love is the best applied logotherapy". Unconditional mutual acceptance and shared faith enable all to mature, to grow, to heal and to be healed. By this kind of love they direct each other constantly to Christ, the Saviour, Sanctifier and Healer.

g) *The sacrament of Ministerial Priesthood*

Through vocation and the sacrament, Christ, Healer and Saviour, establishes a new special relationship with those whom he has chosen to serve his people as deacon, priest or bishop. Just as they are called to proclaim and celebrate the Mystery of Salvation, so are they also meant to embody, in Christ, the synthesis between revealing and healing in both their ministry and, of course, like all the faithful, in their lives.

They can best understand this mission as "wounded healers" touched by the Divine Physician. They must know that they are in need of the Saviour and Healer just as much as all the others, for the self-righteous exclude themselves from being healed and becoming healers in Christ. The priest does not need a mask to hide his wounds and his vulnerability. In the freedom of the children of God, he can acknowledge his shortcomings and confess his sins, since he is grateful for being accepted and affirmed by the Divine Physician. And as he turns to his flock in sympathetic healing love, he likewise needs patient, healing acceptance on the part of all the faithful. Members of the ministerial priesthood are meant to serve in a way which makes the whole community realize the synthesis between revealing and healing and reaches out to all.

6. Faith that drives out demons

The mission entrusted by Christ to his Church entails the driving out of demons or evil spirits. There are many idols, ideologies and evil spirits beleaguering today's humanity. They damage many people's lives and sicken our society and culture. It is through authentic faith that believers unmask all these demons and can gradually drive them out. I think especially of idols like violence, consumerism, growth mania, money mania, the bedevilling of opponents in one's own country and Church, and particularly the mutual bedevilling of international relations threatening mutual destruction. All this takes on demonic dimensions against which diplomacy and psychology — important though they be — are powerless. We need faith, reliance on the power of God.

In a world where God is denied or his Name is taboo, there is ample room for devils and bedevilling. I was surprised to hear in Russia how frequently people raised in atheism make use of expressions like "to the devil with you!" In the pagan world where Christ is still unknown, as well as in the traditionalist context where many precepts and doctrines are known but the Christ of the Gospel is only superficially known, there exists a strange mixture of superstition and fear of evil spirits.

In many tribes and traditionalist cultures there is still a widespread fear of witches and all kinds of witchcraft. Whenever serious affliction comes in the form of sickness, sterility, miscarriage, the death of a beloved one or other calamities, they tremble in fear of evil spirits and look for "evil" men or women who might be agents of the evil spirits (witches), acting out of jealousy, enmity or in vindictiveness. This greatly aggravates their anguish, destroys relationships and creates a pestilent atmosphere of suspicion leading to all kinds of persecution. Innocent people are suspected, persecuted, treated to diabolical abuse and tortured, and forced into making false confessions in a world full of evil cruelty. This is surely an atmosphere in which the "princes of darkness" can use their weaponry of deception and hatred.

As a reaction to all this, in many regions anti-magic processes have been devised, systems of divination to discover the witches, rites and sacrifices meant to detect vicious omens or placate the spirits. Whilst we read about these practices in African, Asian or non-Christian countries,[10] we would do well to take note of similar perversions within Christian groups. A certain kind of ritualism and exorcism came to provide a sort of anti-magic "medicine" for some Catholics: a strange "therapy" somehow caught up in a vortex of collective insanity. How can we meet the genuine cry for help from superstitious and really tormented people, if at the same time we tolerate the practices of magic/anti-magic priests?

I hope the reader will bear with me if I give my personal experience in Bavaria when I was teaching moral theology there over thirty years ago. Many rural people came to our monastery when calamities happened on their farms — trouble with livestock and such. They just asked to have objects blessed, as a kind of immunization. I was frequently called to do this for them and I gradually developed my own "ritual" when I saw that the people harboured suspicions against someone alleged to have been the cause of the calamity. Blessing the objects for them could appear to be an approval of their suspicions, but I did not refuse to give the blessing. I would do it, however, only after a serious catechesis and dialogue, in which I explained that the evil spirits could not enter their barn, their stall or their chamber unless they had opened doors and windows for them. The great doors were suspicion, enmity, bitterness, unforgiveness fostered against their neighbours. The open windows were greed and similar vices. My blessing would help only if they were converted and closed their minds, their hearts and their homes to such evil spirits.

Usually the people would then make a Confession and go home with renewed heart and their objects blessed. When they sensed the blessing this brought them they sent others to me — informing them of my "procedure". What I was trying to do was to awaken in them a healing faith and trust in God and renewed love of their neighbour —

a kind of logotherapy — without refusing to give them the symbols of God's blessing of which they thought so highly. And I am convinced that the liberating, healing activity of the Church should not overlook the value of impressive symbols which stimulate memories that have been healed.

7. Faith-healing

Faith-healing has its historical connotation in the Anglo-American context of revival movements.[11] Within the new movement of Charismatic Renewal it has a much more acceptable meaning, in the sense of what faith can mean for healing and especially for healing relationships.[12]

It is impossible to name a common denominator of the mentalities and phenomena of the various kinds of faith-healing, especially if we include the influential and fast-growing "Healing Churches" of Africa. Much of it is time-bound and culturally conditioned. There is frequently a sound kernel surrounded by enthusiastic exaggerations.

The valuable elements that are found almost everywhere are a high appreciation of prayer as an expression of trust in God, the role of the faith-community, the call to great trust in God's love and power, praise of God for his healing love, and the role of charismatic personalities within a community of believers. The particular cult of a charismatic healer or the ways in which the enthusiasm is expressed may sometimes seem strange. However, this should not keep us from recognizing the value of enthusiastic faith and trust in God, particularly when these lead to the praise of God and an abiding gratitude which permeates the whole of life.

Within the Catholic Charismatic Renewal Movement and in the Neo-Pentecostalism within the Anglican, Lutheran and Methodist Churches, there is frequently — and rightly — more emphasis on the faith-community than on individual healers. The individual charisma is seen within the charisma of the healing community.

There is a harmful tendency, which has still not been fully eliminated, of assuring those who seek healing that they will be healed "if they have enough faith". This is an illegitimate appropriation of the unique prerogative of Jesus to assure a sick person concretely, "Have faith and you will be healed". A harmful side-effect of this is that a sick person who is not healed in spite of his or her faith may feel guilty or not having enough faith or, at least, feel judged so by others.

I will stress some points which distinguish my position from certain tendencies in some healing sects. These sects frequently focus attention on the miraculous, the extraordinary, which is then used apologetically for proving the truth of the sect and/or the miraculous power of their charismatic leaders. For the same reason they look mainly for instantaneous healing. I do not, of course, deny that God can intervene in most extraordinary ways. Our emphasis is not on the miraculous but on the ongoing, progressive healing of persons and relationships, the great impact of the spiritual dimension on the total psychosomatic reality, and the prime importance of the faith-community: the personal faith and trust in God.

But at the same time we can say with Kelsey: "Healing is always a miracle . . . and never more so than when its centre is the greatest of all miracles — love".[13] Faith-healing has its centre in God, who is love. It helps people discover in themselves the image of God. Loving believers awaken in others faith in love, in God, and invite them lovingly to let the Spirit dwell in their hearts. The person who lets love work consciously in his or her whole life is truly on the way to wholeness, integration, healing and is associated with Christ the Healer and the healing community of believers. Faith-healing is an intrinsic factor of the faith-community where all praise the miracles of God's love and where faith bears fruit in love.

My first concern in this book is an all-embracing understanding of salvation and truly human health in a biblical synthesis of the therapeutic nature of the proclamation and the celebration of salvation. And while the charisma of each individual is highly esteemed, there is more emphasis on the inner resources of all, awakened by the Spirit, and the healing of the faith-community in an indispensable manifestation of the solidarity of salvation.

Last but not least, the Church gives and must give great attention to transforming frustrating suffering — insofar as it is expression of a fallen, frustrated world and history — into a redeemed and redeeming suffering. It is the physician's duty to fight against unbearable pain, while it is the grace-endowed mission of the faithful and of the faith-community to discover the deep meaning of suffering in the light of redemption. This was the meaning that gave St Paul "happiness" in his "way of helping to complete, in my poor flesh, the full tale of Christ's suffering still to be endured" (Col 1:24). This discovery and acceptance is truly a way to wholeness, to healing and saving relationships, and brings an important source of strength into the effort to ensure truly human health.

8. Healing and liberating reconciliation with death

The Apostle of the Gentiles crowns his praise of redemption with his hymn on liberation "from the law of sin and death" (Rom 8:2). Unredeemed man, enslaved by psychic and social reinforcements and constantly tormented, is not reconciled to his mortality, his prospect of having to die. He cannot face death with serenity. We are all on the road to death, and by redemption are destined to reach in death a summit of fullness-of-being. But anyone whose outlook on life does not really comprise a positive meaning of death is not able to live an authentic life. He is unable to discover his unique calling and the One who calls him into being and into the fullness of life even in death. His existence is immersed in trivialities; he remains a lonely person in the crowd of depersonalized people.

Whoever, on the contrary, is reconciled to his or her mortality and prepared to die his or her own death in final trust, gains a rich dimension of freedom for living an authentic life and an outlook on life that rings true.[14]

The faith we celebrate and which gives us the grace of salvation and wholeness, the faith that grants us true life, has its deepest roots in the death of Christ which, in synthesis with his resurrection, is the source of our redemeption. Thus we say a saving "Yes" to death in the very act and expectation of resurrection.

Liberated in Christ from the prospect of a meaningless death, we gain a new caring, a new solicitude not only for life but also for that death which is meant for us by God, our Creator and Redeemer: our fulfilment, the day of harvest, our home-coming forever.

This Christian solicitude for a mature death in final trust liberates us for the life here and now, day by day. In the light of death understood with Christ as *kairos*, as the great hour destined by God, the believer discovers in each moment the challenge and unique offer of fruitful living. Through reconciliation with one's mortality in the light of the Paschal Mystery, the door is open also for a liberating understanding of suffering and illness, a door leading to true wholeness and authenticity.

Anyone who is prepared for death understood as the final coming of the Lord and being called home by him will never jeopardize his or her life and health senselessly. The salvation message is a powerful warning against all kinds of unnatural, untimely dying: not only against suicide but also against accidental death caused by lack of responsibility, loss of health and early death through alcoholism and other addictions, including smoking and an unhealthy life-style. Reverence before the Lord of life and death also obliges a more acute ecological consciousness.

Pastors, families, friends and members of the healing and caring professions will find all the right expressions of affirmation, loving care and faith-witness in order to assist the dying in their final "Yes". For this purpose, all should acquire a basic knowledge of the psychology of the dying, the phases through which the sick normally come to their full acceptance and meaning of death. We shall try to understand what the dying are trying to tell us[15] in order to find the appropriate words and gestures of communication.

Reconciled with Brother Death and prepared to die our own death, we can ever better understand what it means for human wholeness and health to be reconciled with God, with one's neighbour and with ourselves. It is in these dimensions that the power of faith shines through.

NOTES:

1. On this point there are some excellent books in German: J. Sudbrack (ed.) *Heilkraft des Glaubens*, Freiburg 1975; J. Hoeren (ed.), *Heilkraft des Glaubens*, Ostfildern 1983; F. Arnold, *Der Glaube, der uns heilt, Zur Therapeutischen Dimension des Christlichen Glaubens*, Regensburg 1983.
2. J. Kovel, *A Complete Guide to Therapy. From Psychoanalysis to Behavior Modification*, New York 1976, p. 148f.
3. C. H. Wolff, *Jesus als Psychotherapeut*, Stuttgart 1978.
4. Cf. E. Bieser, "Heil, als Heilung – Aspekte einer Therapeutischen Theologie", in: J. Sudbrack (ed.), *Heilkraft des Heiligen*, Freiburg 1975, pp. 102–139.
5. B. Hanssler, "Angst und Hoffnung", in: *Artz und Christ* 29 (1983), p. 59.

6. Quoted by F. Arnold from an unedited work of Deutinger: Arnold, *l.c.*, p. 78.
7. This vision is vigorously elaborated by R. A. Lambourne in *Community, Church and Healing*.
8. Cf. St Alphonsus, *Praxis Confessarii*, no. 1 and no. 19.
9. *Constitution on Liturgy*, no. 73.
10. I found it very interesting to read the well-documented book of a former student of mine who, through many years, taught moral theology in African countries and wrote about a great tribe which is also known to me: V. Salvoldi, *Il Banchetto Sacro: Aspetti della Nigeria*, Bologna 1981, pp. 151–175.
11. Cf. J. M. Buckley, *Christian Science, Faith-Healing and Kindred Phenomena*, New York 1982; M. Barbanell, *Saga of Spirit Healing*, London 1954; G. Bishop, *Faith-Healing: God or Fraud?*, Nashville 1967.
12. Cf. F. McNutt, *Healing*, Notre Dame 1974.
13. M. T. Kelsey, *Healing and Christianity*, New York 1973, p. 363.
14. Cf. M. Heidegger, *Sein und Zeit*, Gesamtausgabe Vol. II, Frankfurt 1977, pp. 319, 349, 353.
15. Cf. Kübler-Ross, *Living with Death and Dying*, New York 1981.

CHAPTER SIX

WOUNDED HEALERS IN A WOUNDED AND SICK SOCIETY

The Saviour of mankind is himself the archetype of the "wounded healer". In Christ we see the fulfilment of what Second Isaiah foretold about the Servant of God: "A man of sorrows and familiar with suffering, a man to make people screen their faces . . . And yet ours were the sufferings he bore, our sorrows he carried . . . through his wounds we are healed" (Is 53:3–5). Jesus, the divine and human Physician, is more deeply wounded than any other human being and all his wounds and sufferings are intimately linked with his mission as saviour and healer. The mystery of this utter solidarity between the healer and those to be healed should be seen as the key to authentic healing in a perspective of salvation.

Each Christian can share in his or her own way in the healing ministry of Christ. All are called to enter as completely as possible into the dimension of saving solidarity. But all of us, too, are wounded by our own sins and shortcomings and the more consciously and humbly we accept this fact the better we can heal and help.

In the next two chapters our main attention will be on the healing-caring professions in today's society, and then on Church ministry and the Church-community as a whole.

Healer and patient at one and the same time, each and all of us, are partially contaminated by the various sicknesses in our environment and wounded by the solidarity of sin. Yet we all receive redeeming and healing powers from a saving solidarity in Christ and the more we dedicate ourselves to our redemptive and healing mission the more we can be freed from sin-solidarity.

Members of the healing profession need special attention because not only are they faced constantly with suffering but the very suffering of those for whom they lovingly care touches them deeply, burdens them and can wound them. This is particularly true in cases where psychotherapists enter into a very demanding relationship with their patients. On the occasion of a "transfer" they experience painfully their own wounds and their vulnerability. The sometimes troublesome reactions of a patient can wound them especially because of their deep compassion and dedication. Carl Gustav Jung developed the archetype of the "wounded healer" from his own experience. The archetype indicates symbolically a profound "knowledge about a wound by which the healer suffers with his patient".[1]

Jung emphasizes one of the therapist's risks. The patient's emotions can have a contaminating effect: they find a kind of resonance in the therapist's nervous system, especially during psychoanalysis. As a consequence, psychotherapists and other therapists can become somehow unsettled. This is part and parcel of the transfer whenever there are deep feelings of solidarity between therapist and patient.[2]

This has much to do with Christ, who compassionately bears our burden in order to save us. Healing love strengthens the identity and integrity of the healer or helper, but because of the healer's own wounds all kinds of tensions can arise. Scars not yet fully healed can cause recurrent pain.

1. Dignity and risks of the healing professions

In all religions and cultures the healing professions have enjoyed appreciation and social prestige and as a group they have tried to remain worthy of these honours by upholding and maintaining a high level of a specific ethos.

The healing-helping professions (physicians, psychotherapists, nurses, social workers, child-care personnel, etc.) need to have a considerable degree of altruism, sensitivity and trustworthiness. To the extent that they fulfil their task responsibly and competently, they participate in the redeeming, healing ministry of Christ. But it must be emphasized that, according to the biblical message of redemption, the indispensable call to conversion and renewal includes healers and helpers as well as patients and those in need of help. Also, the institutions geared to healing are in constant need of renewal. All who proclaim salvation and intend to be servants of reconciliation, liberation and healing are in need of the Divine Healer and of mutual support.

Those young men and women, who throughout the ages have

entered in religious communities dedicated to the care of the sick and aged and have generously served the most desperate needs with very restricted means, have known that such a profession requires a great and steadfast idealism. It means nothing less than a vocation to exist-for-others and bear the burden of others. For Christians this means pointing with all one's life to Christ who came to bear our burdens, the Divine-human Physician "through whose wounds we are healed".

The healing professions have much in common with the priestly vocation. In fact, in some cultures these two vocations were often indistinguishable. They existed in a kind of symbiosis, or at least in a profound mutuality of vision and endeavour. Both healers and priests tried to interpret life's deeper meaning in terms of existence in troubled situations. They considered themselves as dedicated to the "sacred".

In the course of increasing differentiation between the healing and the priestly professions there arose, time and again, conflicts, misunderstandings and jealousies between healers and priests.[3] Even professional groups striving for high ideals and a noble ethos are tempted by sin, by the dark powers of the subconscious and of collective egotism. In other words, everyone and everything are in need of redemption and purification.

Within Christianity, which has its focal point in the synthesis of love of God and love of one's neighbour, especially the needy neighbour, the healing-caring-helping professions are highly relevant. Without them, a full testimony to salvation and an integrated proclamation of the Good News are hardly thinkable. But this does not imply either a monopoly of altruism nor a handing over to certain professions, to the extent that others would no longer be called on to heal, to care and to help. These latter, however, should keep in healthy contact with those other professions in a wide range of mutual understanding and collaboration.

In his Apostolic Letter, *Salvifici Doloris* (no. 29), Pope John Paul II pays tribute to all the men and women throughout the world who are dedicated to healing and helping, to overcoming hatred, violence, cruelty, contempt for persons and insensitivity or indifference to sufferers. He stresses the fact that the Church sees them all as workers in solidarity with Christ, the Merciful Samaritan. They live an essential dimension of the Gospel: the irrepressible urge to take action in the face of suffering. We can already hear the words of Jesus on judgment day: "You have done it for me". The day of resurrection will reveal both the redeeming power of suffering in conformity with Christ and the healing love for those who suffer.

All this should make clear how much the members of the healing and helping-caring professions deserve our gratitude, our support and a more appreciative interpretation of their mission in the perspective of the pastoral ministry of the Church. Healers or helpers who in the process of altruistic dedication have become particularly wounded deserve sensitive and therapeutic help from the whole community and especially from competent therapists and priests. A healer who has truly found his home in the faith-community is better able than others who lack such support to burden himself with the risks encountered by vulnerable and wounded healers.

If it is true that physicians and other members of the healing professions often neither seek nor accept timely help for themselves,[4] it is even more tragic if there is any lack of pastoral sensitivity and assistance for those dedicated men and women who spend their best energies in the service of others. A practical question, however, is whether many theologians and pastors are aware of this problem and are competent to fulfil their role in union and co-operation with members of the healing profession.

2. The "helpless helpers"

After all the empirical research that has been done, it is no longer possible to doubt the fact that, in countries where the "health industry" pattern is most developed, the proportion of members of the healing professions working within this system who are plagued by depression and suicidal tendencies is higher than the average in the total population.[5] This is a definite challenge not only to the existing modern technical pattern and the various institutions of "health delivery" but also to theology and the present attitude of pastoral care.

In his book on the "helpless helpers", which has drawn much attention but also some sharp criticism, the psychotherapist Wolfgang Schmidbauer points to the "helper's syndrome" as the main cause of these cases of depression among men and women of the helping and healing professions. He looks for the causes of this in experiences they have had during early childhood which might have triggered off their choice of these professions and a somehow unhealthy approach to them. After many discussions with representatives of social sciences, Schmidbauer takes more carefully into account the social-environmental causes. Therefore, he echoes the call of society, and particularly of these professions, for revision of the present model.

It is not Schmidbauer's intention to belittle or scorn the proven altruism in these professions and among persons who suffer from the "helper's syndrome". On the contrary, he is convinced that the syndrome, in its mild forms, can even reinforce the altruism. The healing is meant to allow a more healthy, more creative and helpful expression of genuine altruism.

In assessing the more serious forms of "helper's syndrome" Schmidbauer does put his finger on one aspect of it, namely, the wounding experiences of the unwanted child or the child submitted to domineering parents, educators or other authority figures, concurrent with an unrealistic idealism. The helper or healer can be obsessed by the thought — in itself right — that those entrusted to "my care" should not suffer "as I did" from a lack of attention and self-assertion and acceptance. However, the overpowering super-ego (heritage of the authoritarian figure) and the suffering resulting from an inability to live coherently at the level of one's high ideal can lead to rigidity towards oneself and towards those under one's care.

These mostly unconscious forces make a healthy mutuality impossible. There is, instead, a one-way relationship. Under the pressure of this syndrome, helpers want to give but do not allow themselves consciously to look for anything in return, such as gratitude, affection or affirmation. They do not seek from the cared-for person the creative and rewarding contribution of co-responsibility, for they are unable to acknowledge to themselves or to their patients that they, too, are wounded and constantly in need of being supported, i.e. in need of mutual regard. Their refusal of conscious recognition of their hunger and thirst for this mutuality — a stance which is even more restless at the unconscious and subconscious level — blocks the way to healthy and healing relations.

The "helper's syndrome" also leads helpers of this kind to a sort of addiction to total dedication to the healing-helping profession while neglecting their private sphere, the needs of their family, themselves and others, needs which are present in a high degree but are not recognized. Thus, the "wounded healer" cannot operate effectively in his or her own personal life.

Schmidbauer, himself a psychoanalyst and therapist, asserts that this danger exists particularly among psychoanalysts and the various schools of psychotherapy, where he has discovered much intolerance, jealousy and distrust. This kind of distrust is reflected unavoidably in the relations between individual therapists.[6]

Helpers who are affected by this syndrome feel themselves in their element with sick people or others entrusted to them if, because of "regressive neuroses", these people like to be "mothered" and tutored. And if one of their patients refuses this kind of relationship, they complain about lack of gratitude, while at other times they like to assure themselves and others that they do not at all depend on gratitude. Another doctor-therapist feels that "it can be observed that nurses find more satisfaction in caring for a totally helpless patient than for one who gradually regains his or her autonomy".[7]

The "helper's syndrome" can be epidemic in psychiatric institutions. Psychiatrists have to look for order and discipline, and are thereby tempted to look only for submissiveness in patients instead of encouraging self-reliance and constructive co-operation.[8]

It is no wonder that this syndrome played a noticeable role within the Church, in a moral and pastoral theology and practice centred on obedience and docility. It produced also authoritarian churchmen, preconditioned to it by their own upbringing. In the Church's activity, as well as in all healing and social professions, a chief criterion is education for freedom: encouragement of growth in responsible, creative freedom. The more our healers, helpers, pastoral workers accept, freely and consciously, their own wounds and shadows, the less will be their danger of falling into the "helper's syndrome" or, at least, its graver forms can be more easily avoided.

A healthy sense of thankfulness, a consciousness that we all are in need of affirmation and acceptance and a gracious kind of helpfulness towards others: all this has a healing power and promotes healthy relationships everywhere. But an imaginary selflessness that makes one feel, "I can serve others but I don't need them", hinders one from reaching a healthy understanding and practice of the commandment, "Love your neighbour as yourself".

The psychiatrist Stanley A. Leavy feels that a main cause of the special susceptibility of many physicians and psychotherapists to this syndrome is their reservation regarding the idea of transcendence. Among others, he mentions Sigmund Freud who followed a widespread trend that denied any authentic experience of a transcendent reality. Declaring any faith in a personal God to be unhealthy and neurotic, he felt obliged to interpret human existence and human health without — and even in opposition to — religion.

No wonder, then, that famous and not-so-famous representatives of the healing profession think that they can set themselves up as little gods. Acting thus, they deprive their patients of co-responsibility and make them believe that they have no freedom. Both Leavy and Menninger speak of atheistic psychoanalysts who boast that, thanks to their treatment, they have freed their patients from religious belief.[9] If this kind of procedure is linked with a philosophy and psychology of self-centred "self-fulfilment", then we are faced with a dangerous contamination of patients by doctors who transfer to them one of the most devastating illnesses of our time.

In the same context Leavy warns representatives of religion that they can damage greatly the psychic health of believers if they do not allow them any kind of doubt about religious matters or their own teaching, thus blocking the inborn desire for sincere search for more light. Whoever, in the name of human authority or even worse in the name of religion, seeks to impose on persons under their care a whole package of doctrines and laws without allowing any personal discernment is surely not a healer. Such people are sick authority figures and spread sickness to others. They can only be healed if they humbly acknowledge their own wounds, ills and insensitivity.

3. Senior citizens as "wounded healers"

In all its manifold expressions, cheerful caring is a privileged dimension of the healing mission. It prevents many psychic wounds, cures others and has many positive psychosomatic values. It is particularly beneficial in caring for the aged.

Care for senior citizens presents a serious social problem in our urban industrial society with its high proportion of nuclear families. Retirement, being cut off suddenly from their everyday working environment and habits while still in good physical and psychic health, finds many people unprepared to use and enjoy their leisure time. They feel lost, empty. There can be a painful feeling of being no longer of use to anyone, a feeling of isolation and loneliness. Others, relegated to nursing homes, feel exiled from their former homes, neglected by their relatives and friends. There is also the gradual experience of more and more discomfort from failing sight, hearing and mobility as they reach the final stages of life. All this cries out to the Church, as well as to society, for healing and caring — for the "good Samaritan".[10]

The Church is now discovering that the senior citizens themselves can be an almost inexhaustible reservoir of "Samaritans", wounded healers who, like the "elders" of the earliest Christian tradition, are willing and able to bring their life-experience and their generosity creatively into the life of the community. This is true for both men and women. The decline in traditional priestly vocations is a challenge to the Church to rediscover in a new way the rich potential of gifted "elders". A high percentage of those who now retire around their sixtieth year could and should be prepared to share in the mission of the Church, to proclaim the Good News, to heal and to care.

Both Church and society have to revise their ideas about the elderly. A first response is to offer them ample opportunity for ongoing education. Our society is greatly mistaken if it neglects this simply because it might not repay on the market. This very attitude is one of the destructive illnesses of our society — that it measures values by rules of the market, while missing so many things of higher value.

Ongoing education could be an interdisciplinary endeavour to communicate and deepen our own insights on aging, the role of the elderly, their problems and potentialities. As a result, we would find that persons of this age-group are not only able to recognize better their own situation but can also help others to solve their problems in a creative way and put their capacities at the service of those aging persons who are most in need.

The Church should offer some preparatory training to senior citizens willing to help in the pastoral care of the aged and lonely. According to the letter of St James the "elders" can pray for and with the sick and suffering, bless them, allow them to talk trustfully of their past failings, and bring to them the joy of faith (cf. Jas 5:14). The question of whether these elders of today could be ordained for administering the sacrament of Anointing could easily be resolved, but in any case they could be the ones best able to prepare their contemporaries for the consolation of the sacraments.

Enlisting the activity of our senior citizens would mean that many ageing persons could be spared isolation in poorly-run old folks homes. In various parts of the world, senior citizens have already organized regular visits to the lonely — visits which aim at consoling, cheering-up, helping and bringing the Good News of healing love.

A modern revival of the ancient institute of the "elders" and "widows" could bring new resources to the whole pastoral and healing mission of the Church. And this could mean that many people would find their highest fulfilment, in the last decades of their life, by becoming helpers of the Divine Healer.

4. The family: solidarity of "wounded healers"

Social and humane sciences have studied the manifold interactions of individual, family, cultural and socio-economic life. The interactions within the family and of the family within its total environment powerfully affect each other. The good and healthy elements, but also the weaknesses and wounds of individual family members affect the whole family, while the family as a unit has its own particular influence on the world around it. The environment can be a great threat and danger, especially for those families which have not realized their shared responsibilities.

In the Christian vision, the family is called to be a salvific community dedicated to the wholeness, integrity and salvation of each member. And the family as a united whole can prove to be for many other people a sort of "sacrament" through the example it gives of healing solidarity. But it is itself vulnerable in the initial relations of its members and in its reciprocity to the outside world. The more the family dedicates itself to healing wounds and reconciling people, the more it can — as a "wounded healer" — withstand the contagious powers within and around itself.

The greatest healing power of the family is the mutual love of its members, which means mutual affirmation, faithfulness, and readiness to forgive and to be reconciled. This is the most successful "logotherapy".

The social professions and their respective institutions are mostly busy repairing damages and wounds which arise within the families or afflict them through the unhealthy world around them. This poses question to Church and society, namely, "Are we doing enough to keep families healthy and to sensitize them to their responsibility to become healthy and healing powers for their environment, for society and for the State? Are we doing enough to create good economic, social and cultural conditions for them? Is enough being done to prepare the young generation for marriage and family life?"

If all the members of the social service and healing professions receive the necessary formation and support, they can do much to assist and to heal sick and endangered families and can thereby learn much that will make for a creative contribution to their own families. But, as we have seen in our reflection on the "helper's syndrome", they can be so preoccupied with helping others that they may gravely neglect their own families and their most intimate relationships.

It is possible for a professional career, even that of the healing and helping, to take over completely to the detriment of everyone involved. But it is not true healing or helping activity if it becomes a flight from one's own problems and one's own family. Typical might be the statement of a doctor: "Since my wife does not find an acceptable solution for fertility control, she refuses to sleep with me. I am hurt, but I don't tell her. So I feel much more at ease in the clinic and go home late".[11] The wife complains that her husband has no time for her. She feels jealous of her husband's patients and becomes increasingly critical, which drives the husband still further into absorption in his professional activity.

Worse still is the situation when one partner is so much a slave of a success-oriented culture that he lets himself become totally absorbed by his drive for more and more money, his only idea of "success". This is part of the sickness of Western cultures, with their mania for amassing more and more stimulated, by manipulative advertising that lures families into ever increasing consumption. Spending and pressure to purchase intrude more and more on family life. Spouses have no time for each other; parents have no time for their children, and instead of giving themselves to them they load them with material gifts. Add to all this the prevailing individualistic world-view whereby each one thinks in terms of his or her own "self fulfilment"! This, too, can become an addiction and a cause of other addictions.

Strained relationships cause many kinds of psychosomatic disorders and can ravage one's spiritual well-being. If a family, exposed to these risks, begins to understand itself as a healing community and each member sees his or her role as a "wounded healer", these dangers can usually be avoided.

In marriage and in the family people meet and live in a profound, indissoluble mutuality. Each person contributes positive energies and healing powers, but also some provocative and hurtful "shades". Anyone who enters on marriage dreaming of an idyll of life with an absolutely ideal partner is heading for a rude awakening. From the outset, then, it is the task of man and wife to love each other as each really is, accepting good points and defects. This can succeed all the more easily if each spouse admits to being a "wounded" person and, therefore, in need of a healer, but is aware at the same time of being a "healer" with powerful inner strengths for both self-healing and for encouraging the other to discover similar interior resources. This means a firm "Yes" by husband and wife to be, each for the other, healer for the "wounded healer" "until death do us part".

The opposite choice is the futile and frustrating game of "if only", "yes, but".[12] Such poor players are victims of feelings of helplessness, impotent yearnings, a desire to be cared for, "mothered", while at the same time making affirmation by the partner almost impossible. Therapy is not easy, but such people are in dire need of help. A first step is to help them to understand the hideous goings on of the forces they are releasing. What has been said in the previous chapter about the healing power of the biblical virtues can be helpful in therapy here.

5. Alcoholics Anonymous as "wounded healers"

For an apt example of "wounded healer" in today's society we can look to members of Alcoholics Anonymous. They have the courage to tell their story, to acknowledge their wounds and failures. They let the other know that "I am not any better than you", but they also tell gratefully the good story of how they found strength through help from other anonymous alcoholics. They share the profound conviction that "If I, with all my scars, could do it, surely you can, too!"

This model is no longer restricted to the healing of alcoholics; its powerful dynamics are transplanted into other fields as well. My own experience of being completely larynxectomized gives me a unique opportunity to help others who are already or may soon be in the same situation. Those especially who, like myself, experience drawbacks should be encouraged not to give up, but to muster their inner resources of strength to discover a deeper meaning for their readjustment. It is well known that the best helpers of cancer patients can be others who have experienced the same problems and are still faced with them. It is to be hoped that both doctors and the Church will learn to mobilize these "wounded healers".

6. "Wounded healers" and the healing of public life

Healing of public life is one of the great themes and dimensions of social ethics. Here, only some aspects need attention. We all suffer in one way or another under the evils, disorders and dangerous, contagious trends of our surroundings, our socio-economic society and culture. None of us is free from all the pitfalls. There are two aspects of the situation and we can become constructive in our critical efforts, our proposals and co-operation only when we face both of them, namely, that we can and must work for the healing of at least some facets of public life, and that we, too, are affected by the virus, are wounded and are part of the problem.

It we really commit ourselves to some effort for a healthier public life, we have to start not only talking — important as dialogue may be — but also doing. For instance, as soon as it became clear that smoking was the most important single factor in developing lung cancer and for poor prospects of overcoming it, many doctors stopped smoking almost immediately. They felt that, as doctors, they would lose credibility in their own eyes as well as in the eyes of their patients if they continued to smoke as though they were unaware of the dangers. If a doctor is not willing or not able to stop, he will not have the courage, generally speaking, to tell a patient frankly, "Your disease is your heavy smoking". Rather, he will prefer to turn a blind eye to the link between them.

If we commit ourselves, together with others, to the healing of public life in some of the most urgent aspects of our sick culture — consumerism, corrupt politics and so on — we will discover gradually our own share, our own complicity in the sickness, although heretofore it might have been hidden from our conscience.

Members of the healing and helping professions need to have, and often do have, a certain amount of room for giving gratuitous services over and above the demands of today's mentality which values only what can be paid for. Their dedication to the sick and needy where they can expect no remuneration or compensation is of great value in the healing of one particular dimension of our contemporary culture. Schmidbauer, whom I have quoted in connection with his research on the "helper's syndrome", is very conscious of the genuine altruism in these professions. "Modern industrial society is beginning to suffer so much under the constraints of quantitative growth and progress that it is forced to allow gaps where its value-system is dispensed with. And I think that real changes will take place within these gaps".[14]

For these reasons, and many others, it is regrettable that vocations for the healing and helping professions in religious life are becoming rare. Religious Orders should be sharply aware that they too have a mission for healing public life. Their members, almost unavoidably, are "wounded" to some extent, contaminated by the sickness of the culture. But becoming fully conscious of this and trusting in the healing power of Christ through faith, they can become more effective healers, while never denying to either themselves or others that they are, just like others, "wounded healers".

NOTES:

1. Cf. C. G. Jung, *Die Dynamik des Unbewussten*, Gesammlete Werke, vol. 8, 2nd ed., Freiburg 1977; id., *Praxis der Psychotherapie*, Ges. Werke, vol. 16, 2nd ed., Freiburg 1976; H. J. Nowen, *The Wounded Healer*, New York 1972; C. J. Groesbeck, "Der Archetypus des verwundeten Arztes" in: J. Sudbrack (ed.), *Heilkraft des Heiligen*, Freiburg 1975, pp. 177–208.
2. Cf. C. G. Jung, *Analytic Psychology*, New York 1968.
3. This theme is well treated in M. E. Marty and K. Vaux, *Health, Medicine and the Faith Traditions*, pp. 53–162.
4. Cf. W. Schmidbauer, *Die Hilflosen Helfer. Über die Seelische Problematik der Helfenden Berufe*, Reinbek, 10th ed. 1981, p. 21.
5. *l.c.*, pp. 14–23 with biography.
6. W. Schmidbauer, *l.c.*, pp. 146–152.
7. J. Willi, *Zweierbeziehung*, Reinbek 1975, p. 96.
8. W. Schmidbauer, *l.c.*, p. 161.
9. S. A. Leavy, "Questioning Authority: The Contribution of Psychoanalysis to Religion", in *Crossroad* 32 (1982), pp. 129–142.
10. Cf. E. W. Marvin, *Planning for the Elderly*, Philadelphia 1978; A. Fontana, *The Last Frontier. Social Meaning of Growing Old*, London 1977.
11. Cf. Schmidbauer, *l.c.*, p. 82.
12. Cf. E. Berne, *Games People Play*, New York, 1964.
13. I have dedicated to this theme the major part of volume III of my work, *Free and Faithful in Christ* (St Paul Publications, Slough).
14. W. Schmidbauer, *l.c.*, p. 229f.

CHAPTER SEVEN

THE CHURCH: A WOUNDED HEALER

The main concern of all our reflections in this book is the Church's full mission to proclaim the Gospel of salvation and peace and to heal. We mean the Church in all her dimensions: the people of God, the teaching and learning Church, the Church as pilgrim, the celebrating Church and every facet of the proclaiming and healing Church — and all this as a "wounded healer".

1. The healing power of wounded priests

All the faithful together make up the "priestly people of God"; all are called and enabled to "adore God in spirit and truth". Such adoration has in itself the most potent healing energies. Here, however, we speak of the ministerial priesthood, including the pope, the bishops, priests and deacons, whose most noble and indispensable task is to strive as pastors, together with all the faithful, to become ever more truly "adorers in spirit and truth", thus to be light of the world and salt to the earth.

In common with the healing professions, priests have many opportunities for healing but they are also exposed to certain risks, as we saw in the previous chapter. The more conscious they are of being at one and the same time wounded and vulnerable as well as gifted with healing powers, the more the Saviour and Divine Healer will make them partners in his mission to proclaim the Saving News and to heal.

As a member of the theological community, I think first of the "wounded theologian". Theologians have to be men or women filled with compassion, ready to suffer and to be misunderstood in the fulfilment of a prophetic role, and sharply aware of their vulnerability. They must be alert to the danger of allowing themselves to be contaminated by a vague spirit of the era, by the harmful trends of contemporary culture and by a desire for tranquillity when they ought to dare the stormy sea in order to meet Jesus there.

The theologian must be especially aware that he and his theology are sick if it lacks pastoral mindedness, the dynamic to heal and to reconcile, to unmask ideologies and to reveal the true image of God. Theologians and priests and bishops formed by them can be dangerously contaminated by a morale of success within a success-oriented culture and educational system, or by an ethic of law and mere obedience combined with an unchecked authoritarian-type super-ego — a bowing before those who can remunerate or promote, while downgrading at a lower level.

I can think of theologians who were or are sincere searchers of truth, zealous for people's salvation, dedicated to a therapeutic theology, and yet felt victimized by this kind of theology when they were treated badly by authorities who misunderstood them. They can be so deeply wounded as to become timid or even bitter, sometimes to the point of being unable to heal others.

We see before us a great company of zealous priests who are wearing themselves out physically, psychically, spiritually, in continuous activity for their flock. The syndrome of activity increases under the pressure of a society for which the bigger the output the higher the praise deserved. Add to this a great exodus of dissatisfied, frustrated priests who, by their example, discourage priestly vocations!

Many are wounded so deeply because they do not grasp the authentic identity of their vocation and are unable to discern the signs of the times. Some have received an unbalanced formation marked by legalism in moral theology, formalism in liturgy and a static view of the Church. With such a mentality how can they feel at home in a Church which, according to the Second Vatican Council, sees herself as a pilgrim Church? There are also priests who accept sincerely the Pastoral Constitution on the Church, *Gaudium et Spes*, but are unable, and not helped, to find an interpretation of ministerial priesthood corresponding to it. In their conclusion, many find it difficult to accept the co-responsibility and co-operation of lay people.

In all of us there is a hidden "atheist" who wounds and threatens us. Here I think especially of the kind of atheism which has found its classical expression in Ernst Bloch. He denies the existence of a personal God, Creator and Redeemer, because he refuses to be a recipient of gifts that put him under an obligation of indebtedness. Activists, who not only neglect the spiritual-contemplative dimension of faith but also place more trust in their work than in God's grace, stress their own achievements and demand remuneration for everything in one form or another. In reality, their attitude is the counterpart of Bloch's postulatory atheism, but not so coherent and not so conscious of playing at being God.

Priests of all ranks who are addicted to activism can suffer severe forms of the "helper's syndrome". Spending their energy and time for others, they expect nobody to contradict them, nobody to refuse the kind of dependence they want to impose on others. They do not realize that, just as much as those entrusted to them, they need to be grateful recipients; they need affirmation, encouragement and correction in order to remain whole and healthy.

Under the impact of certain structures and expectations many priests, especially those in the higher ranks, do not achieve an organic synthesis and healthy differentiation between their office and their person.

All these wounds can be aggravated by a hurtful "transfer", especially towards people with regressive neuroses who evade personal responsibility and seek security in total subservience to the priest. This happens particularly if the priest is dominated by his super-ego and an authoritarian concept of his role. Since he is not aware of being a wounded person, both he and the one he is relating to become more unhealthy, less capable of healthy and healing relationships.

Another kind of wound is marked by a wavering between ambition and resignation. The more intense the ambition, fed by the environment and by an acknowledged system of promotion and "persona" cult, the more desperate can be, by way of reaction, the urge to resign and to succumb to depression.

What priests need is to have the courage to face up to their vulnerability and to the fact that they are in various ways wounded persons, to put their trust in the Divine Healer and to join him humbly in the double mission of messengers of salvation and ministers of healing. This requires an acute awareness of mutuality and a humble readiness to receive as well as to give in all their dealings with others.

2. A wounded Church in a wounded culture and society

Faced with the problems of the institutional and structural dimensions of the Church in interaction with society and culture, we do not allow ourselves to escape into a disembodied image of the Church. We love the real Church in spite of her imperfect institutions, practices, laws and dependencies. But on the other hand, we do not forget that in all her dimensions, even those of administration and organization, the Church is called to be and should become ever more a "sacrament of salvation and healing". Her entire life in all its facets should point to Christ, the Saviour and Healer. This does not happen automatically. If there is not an ongoing renewal and healing, some institutional elements can even become counter-signs of her true self.

The Second Vatican Council meditated deeply on the mutual relationships and interactions between Church and world, receiving and giving,[1] and on the complex relationship between the proclamation of salvation and culture.[2]

Through her dedicated endeavour to bring about an ever new inculturation of her message, her institutional forms, theological and liturgical language (including symbols and signs) and philosophy in all the living cultures of the inhabited earth ("oikumene"), the Church in turn acquires an enormous store of cultural wealth. Inculturation, together with ongoing dialogue, counteracts the dangers of enshrining the mystery of faith in one single set of formulations, thus losing contact with the life of the people and — this is the most dangerous sickness — forgetting that the mystery of salvation remains infinitely greater than the capacity of any human language. The very effort to ensure uniformity of doctrine through the use of a single dead language destroys the vitality of the salvation message and its healing-saving power within the dynamics of salvation history.

Local Churches, which unhesitatingly work at inculturation but do not maintain contact and dialogue with the centre of the Church and with other local Churches of other cultures, will easily become a prey to cultural narrowness. They are unable to distinguish competently between the abiding truth and the set formulation of them in the past. A totally centralized Church government was no better off when it lived in alliance with just one culture or one language group and in exclusive dependence on it.

The great schisms from the eleventh to the sixteenth century and the splitting-up of the Protestant Church into numerous separate denominations were largely due to cultural, social and political causes. The less conscious churchmen were of the destructive effect of an organic liaison with an individual narrow political and cultural system, the more devastating was the impact of the very diversity of such individual choices of cultural and political systems in perpetuating alienation and enmity. In such circumstances what is in reality an ossification of past adaptations (some authentic and some less acceptable) becomes sacralized and a cause of entrenchment and intolerance. That is why Pope John XXIII rightly urged the Council to spare no pains in working out the distinction between the abiding essence of revealed truth and its various time-bound and culturally-conditioned expressions[3] — a task which is anything but easy.

In her relations with cultures, ecomonic systems, philosophies and styles of authority, the Church must be constantly aware that these are all part and parcel of a world in need of redemption and only in fact redeemed insofar as it is open to Christ, the Saviour, Healer and Servant. Moreover, the Church herself, in her members, her structures, her use of philosophies and ideologies, while proclaiming the salvation message, can be more or less wounded and contaminated by the world around her and by the very historical-cultural means she uses to accomplish her mission. This contamination becomes acute where "sacred alliances between throne and altar" try to perpetuate past systems and privileges and where openness to the signs of the times is lacking.

Each adaptation is imperfect and unavoidably brings with it the need of self-criticism as new historical dimensions arise calling for new and fresh encounters. Well-known examples are the uncritical acceptance of patriarchal family and social structure, an authoritarian monarchy or oligarchies.

When, partially under the very impact of the dynamics of revealed truth, new horizons open up, new symptoms of a "wounded Church" appear. They include new adaptations uncritically accepted and an equally uncritical clinging to an ossified past or imperfect inculturations. This polarization is worse still when ideological justifications are put forward in the name of Revelation.

The transition from a patriarchal family and an authoritarian society to a partnership family and democracy is not easy. In the process of discerning the "signs of the times" painful tensions and polarizations arise. On the one hand, there are those wounded by an anti-authoritarian "spirit of the era"; on the other hand, there are those who were quite happy with their authoritarian education and a male-dominated Church regimentation, so much so that the slightest changes come as a shock, even such things as the appearance of "altar girls" alongside "altar boys". Another example is the painful polarization between those who approve of the arms race "for the defence of our culture" and those who, with great conviction, stand by non-violent defence as the only alternative for survival with dignity.

We all need deep faith and humility, trust in God and sharp awareness of our own vulnerability in order to fulfil our vocation of healing and reconciliation within today's Church and society.

Since the Second Vatican Council the Church has grown in awareness of her wounds and of the need for healing and renewal. The World Council of Churches, too, gives much attention to the fact of a wounded, divided Christianity in a wounded, lacerated world. Healing is urgent and possible if we put our trust in our Saviour. If the various encrustments and cultural constraints are recognized for what they are, wounds can be more easily healed; ecumenical dialogue can become more humble and promising. For all sections of Christianity it will become easier to resist the temptation to absolutize man-made traditions and let them block the road to unity.

The Sixth Plenary Assembly of the World Council of Churches in 1983 strongly emphasized "healing and reconciliation". There was a special commission on "sharing and healing". Painfully, the representatives of large sections of Christianity took note of "the fact that the Churches have no yet sufficiently advanced in being a fellowship of confessing, of learning, of participation, of sharing, of healing, and of reconciliation, to overcome the stumbling blocks which have deeply divided them".[4]

This is the sorry situation of a "wounded healer". But it is much less deplorable than the attitude of past centuries, since now the Churches recognize and humbly confess their shortcomings and their wounds and are in quest of healing in a new mutuality. There are better chances of receiving attention and trust from a badly wounded world when Christian Churches speak humbly and without self-righteousness, as "wounded healers" who draw our attention to the Divine Saviour.

3. Healing from a wounded authority-style

As we saw earlier, the proclamation of the kingdom of God through Jesus is inseparable from his new authority as the "Servant" of God and of men. Hence, sharing in Christ's healing mission is unthinkable without joining Christ in his authority as the Servant.

In his book, "The Five Wounds of Holy Church",[5] Rosmini, one of the greatest Catholic thinkers and reformers of the last century, points particularly to the wounded Church government. He considers the "wound of the left hand" of the crucified Church as the alienation of the clergy, its segregation from the people, which itself is strikingly evident in the public cult (liturgy). He sees the "wound of the right hand" as the inadequate formation of the clergy, which alienates the priests from the rest of the faithful. The "wound of the heart" is the lack of unity and collegiality among priests and bishops, and the "wound of the left foot" is the alienated and alienating appointment of bishops.

Rosmini considers the co-operation of the clergy and faithful in the election of their bishop "a divine right", explicitly acknowledging, however, that the modality must be determined according to the needs and possibilities of time and place. With astonishing frankness he deplores the appointment of local bishops, by the central authority, with a total elimination of the co-operation of the local clergy and faithful. In his eyes, this centralizing mentality was often accountable for simoniacal manoeuvres but his emphasis is on his battle against the appointment of bishops through emperors, kings and princes: rulers of people.

This was the main reason why the Habsburg party considered Rosmini a most dangerous man. It did everything to discredit him and succeeded in getting the Roman Inquisition to put his book on the Index.

The "wound of the right foot" is caused by assaults on the freedom of the Church. Rosmini offers as the most effective remedies freedom from earthly powers, from compromising alliances of throne and altar, and frankness within the Church. For the Church's inner freedom he counts evangelical poverty as the most urgent curative, in view of the Church's earthly possessions and their alienation from their original purpose. Repeatedly he insists that the Church does not need treasures and privileges but rather the freedom to live her own identity and to fulfil her mission faithfully, trusting in her Saviour. With reference to the spirit of poverty, Rosmini holds that regular public accounting of the Church's holdings, income and expenditure is an indispensable remedy for her own healing and credibility: "How well would the Church win the hearts of the faithful by doing so!"[6]

It would be a drastic misunderstanding to fasten the proverb: "Physician, heal yourself" on Rosmini's approach. He was working in utter sincerity to awaken this consciousness in the Church so that, aware of being wounded and needing healing, she would become better able to perform both her role as messenger of salvation and her ministry of healing. Thus, the Church would enjoy an ever-increasing integrity and holiness. He directs our attention to Jesus, **the Divine-human Healer and Saviour**, and urges us to allow Jesus to heal us so that we can become more effectively the "salt to the earth".

Rosmini warns the "yes-men" and flatterers who tell churchmen that everything is all right and whatever they do is excellent. Even more so does he warn those who surround themselves with yes-men who "cover up the wounds, if I may so put it, with 'diplomatic hypocrisy' ".[7]

From Rosmini we can learn a great lesson for our times: a synthesis of frankness and humility, readiness to suffer with the Church and for the Church, a great love of the Church and her leaders, and **a burning desire that the Church may faithfully fulfil her healing ministry as a humble "wounded healer"**.

4. Healing through a healthy life-style

The authority style which Rosmini so frankly and eloquently recommends for healing the five wounds of Church is part of a broader concept of a healthy and healing life-style. We speak here of the whole people of God and their mission to be the "light for the world".

James McGilvray is right in holding that "our life-style is the one factor which exercises the most decisive influence on our health".[8] Hence, the Church's healing ministry obliges her to educate believers in this respect for the sake of health, wholeness and salvation.

What a healthy life-style is with regard to nutrition, sleep, balance between work and leisure, meaningful use of leisure, physical exercise, refreshing contact with nature, development of a sense of beauty, and all such matters, can be learned from competent representatives of the various professions — physicians, therapists, dieticians and others. But more important are the many dimensions and aspects which faith helps us to uncover. Most vital is the development of the contemplative dimension of our existence. Through faith and contemplation we learn how to discern real from artificial needs, acquire a taste for simplicity and gain inner external freedom. We are freed from greed and desire for power and from useless worries, and thus made free for joy in the Lord. Our freedom comes through surrender to the Holy Spirit who teaches us from within ourselves the liberating and healing power of love of God and neighbour and purity of heart in all our relationships. An all-pervading spirit of thanksgiving for the gifts of creation and redemption will motivate us to keep the earth habitable and attractive, to care for a healthy and beautiful environment.

As Christians, we shall not care excessively for our own health, important though it is, but we must in our life-style respond to our mission to be healers for others. Faith in Christ's sacrifice, the simplicity of his being one-of-us, the Servant of all, gives us clear direction and motivation for the right kind of living that must be ours. The life-style of believers, particularly of those who are fully aware of their noble mission to share the Good News and to heal the sick, has to be convincing and attractive in the eyes of all reasoning people.

5. Healing lepers and being healed from our "leprosies"

The invitation to be the first lecturer in the Blessed Peter Donders Chair was a precious occasion for me to engage in deeper reflections about the synthesis of evangelization and healing. It seems therefore appropriate to conclude with a thought on healing leprosy, by way of honouring that great apostle of the lepers.

The healing love of Jesus for lepers, his nearness to them, is a striking feature of Christ's revealing and healing presence. A grateful memory for this part of the Gospel message impels Christ's disciples and messengers to do whatever is in their power to heal humankind from this terrible disease and its devastating consequences, particularly now that this is really possible. Medicine has given us the necessary key to fighting leprosy successfully. The question now is whether, as Christians, we shall use the keys which Christ has given us — healing love, generosity of commitment and the spirit of sacrifice — to eradicate it completely.

Much has to be done. We know that it is not enough to provide the relatively inexpensive medications and to find the contaminated persons in time to offer effective treatment. There is need to provide an overall healthy environment and a healthy diet, especially for the children and all who are exposed to contamination. In the effort to fight leprosy, we face all the problems of the Third World: holistic development, healthy socio-economic and international relations, a common effort for effective co-operation and the promotion of co-responsibility at all levels.

The crusade against leprosy should be conducted in the spirit of the "wounded healer". While our eyes and our hearts are opened to the pitiful situation of the lepers, we can and must open our eyes likewise to our own no less pitiable "leprosies": our dependence on artificially created needs, our many and various addictions, our greed which devours a vastly disproportionate share of the world's riches, our materialistic ideologies. All these and other "leprosies" carry the risk of a gradually induced spiritual vacuum, an existential emptiness that can cause a thousand ills.

The crusade against leprosy right on to its total elimination would take a decade or perhaps several. It should go hand in hand with an awakening consciousness of the greater evils which threaten humanity: the lust for power and possessions, violence, war, enmity, the loss of a simple, serene style of life. The pictures which show the appalling destruction wrought by leprosy should be meditated together with the no less alarming results of alcoholism, drug addiction and terrorism — symptoms of our sick culture.

Our contributions towards wiping out leprosy should be at least partially the harvest of our newly-acquired liberation for the living of a simple life in regard to eating, drinking, housing, travelling and so on. We should no longer be on the look-out for what else we might need but for the many things which we well can do without.

Take just one area: if priests and religious would give-up smoking, alcoholic drink, avoid over-eating, and contribute all they thus save to the healing of leprosy, what energies would be set free for entering into joy of the Lord, proclaiming the Good News, and for healing! How many healthier years would be added to the lives of priests and religious who are so badly needed! While the results would be marvellous for the lepers of the world, they would be even greater for so many people who are threatened by alcoholism and drug addiction and for smokers who are making their way towards lung cancer. Those who up to now have not succeeded in freeing themselves from their addictions, would find a stimulating example and strong motivation.

I mention just one example which struck me when a priest told me his story. He was a zealous priest but an addicted smoker who had not succeeded in helping a good young man overcome a habit of frequent masturbation. In a moment of generosity he said to the young man: "With my habit of smoking, I am no better than you. So, to help you, I promise to stop smoking from now on. You pray for me to be able to fulfil my promise and I will pray for you". The "miracle" happened; each was healed of his habit.

The paradigm of the "wounded healer" means solidarity, mutuality. In taking generous action for the elimination of leprosy, we should implore lepers all over the world to pray for us that our society may become fully aware of its dangerous and contagious diseases and find strength to overcome them — diseases like wastefulness, greed, exploitation, injustice to poor countries and the poor in our own countries, and the pollution of consciences by a sick culture.

The liberation of humankind from leprosy and similar evils is possible but not without the mustering of our inner resources. As we persevere in our efforts on behalf of the lepers and all those who are threatened by contamination, our own energies will assuredly be stimulated, our own consciences sharpened and we shall gain strength in our endeavour to free ourselves and our culture more and more from the diseases of our own time and place, especially from violence, the arms race and all forms of terrorism.[9]

NOTES:

1. *Gaudium et Spes*, nos. 40–44.
2. *l.c.*, nos. 58, 62; *Ad Gentes*, passim.
3. *AAS* 54 (1962), p. 792; *Gaudium et Spes*, no. 62.
4. P. Potter, "A House of Living Stones", in *The Ecumenical Review* 35 (1983), 350–364, quote pp. 361/2.
5. A. Rosmini, *Delle Cinque Piaghe della Santa Chiesa*, written 1832, published 1848, new critical edited by C. Riva, Brescia, 3rd ed., 1967.
6. *l.c.*, ch. V, no. 162.
7. *l.c.*, ch. IV, no. 109.
8. J. McGilvray, *l.c.*, p. 125.
9. I have made these proposals already in my publication: *The Healing Ministry of the Church in the Coming Decades*, CARA, Washington D.C. 1982, p. 19ff.